D0119829

BILL BIRKETT

EXPLORING

40 easier circular walks

THE LAKES &

in the lake district

LOW FELLS 1

David & Charles

This book was produced in association with

JENNINGS
BROTHERS PLC
ESTD 1828

The author would like to acknowledge the generous sponsorship of Jennings Brothers. Located at Cockermouth by the river Cocker, on the edge of the Lake District, Jennings have been brewing beer for over 170 years. Their real ales can be found in inns throughout the Lake District National Park. Conveniently, many of the walks in this book pass by these traditional watering holes.

TO THE LOCALS OF LAKELAND – A HARDY BREED

Photographs on page 1 (clockwise from top left): Over Shingle Point, Buttermere, Walk 28; Grisedale, Walk 39; River Mite, Miterdale, Walk 24; Spring cherry blossom; Autumn blackberries; To Fairfield, from Loughrigg, Walk 2; Waterfalls, Stickle Ghyll, Walk 8; Lily Tarn, Loughrigg, Walk 2.

A DAVID & CHARLES BOOK

All photographs from the Bill Birkett Photo Library

Maps by Martin Bagness based on pre-1950 Ordnance Survey maps. Completely redrawn 2000.

First published in the UK in 2001
Copyright © Bill Birkett 2001

ISBN 0 7153 1077 1

Book design by Diana Knapp
Printed in China by Leefung-Asco
for David & Charles Publishers
Brunel House   Newton Abbot   Devon

CONTENTS

CONTENTS   CONTENTS   CONTENTS   CONTENTS

AREA MAP AREA MAP AREA MAP AREA MAP AREA MAP

Difficulty rating: ● EASY   ● MODERATE   ● DIFFICULT

THE WALKS

1. Ambleside's High to Low Sweden Bridge – 5km/1¾ hours
2. Loughrigg's Lily Tarn above Ambleside – 5km/1¾ hours
3. The Round of Rydal Water – 6km/2½ hours
4. To Alcock Tarn above Grasmere – 5km/2 hours
5. High Close and Hunting Stile above Langdale and Grasmere – 4km/1½ hours
6. A circuit of Elter Water beneath the Langdales – 8km/3½ hours
7. Lingmoor Fell from Chapel Stile – 7km/2½ hours
8. Stickle Tarn descending by Horse Intake and Mill Gill – 3.5km/2 hours
9. Over Holme Fell by Hodge Close and Yew Tree Tarn – 5km/2½ hours
10. Wray Castle by the shores of Windermere Lake – 5.5km/2 hours
11. Hawkshead Heights – 6km/2 hours
12. To Claife Heights from Far Sawrey – 8km/3 hours
13. Around Troutbeck's Tongue – 13km/5 hours
14. Orrest Head above Windermere – 2km/1¼ hours
15. Scout Scar from Helsington Church – 8km/2½ hours
16. Around the Vale of Winster – 9km/3½ hours
17. By Selside and Bethecar Moor above Coniston Water – 6km/3¾ hours
18. Torver Back Common and Coniston Shore – 6km/2½ hours
19. By Broughton's Appletree Worth and the River Lickle – 5.5km/1½ hours
20. Seathwaite Tarn from the Duddon's Birks Bridge – 9km/3 hours
21. Ulpha Park above the Duddon – 10km/2½ hours
22. The circuit of Devoke Water – 5km/1½ hours
23. Stanley Gill falling to the River Esk – 4.5km/2½ hours
24. Miterdale and the stone circles of Burnmoor – 11km/4 hours
25. Port Ravenglass: where the Esk meets the sea – 9km/4 hours
26. Wasdale Head – 4km/2 hours
27. Around Loweswater – 6km/3 hours
28. The round of Buttermere – 7km/3 hours
29. The head of Borrowdale: Seatoller to Seathwaite – 5.5km/2½ hours
30. Castle Crag rising from the Jaws of Borrowdale – 6km/2 hours
31. Derwentwater Heights: by Castlerigg to Walla Crag – 8.5km/3 hours
32. Latrigg above Keswick – 8km/3 hours
33. Castlerigg stone circle to Low Naddle Fell – 6.5km/2½ hours
34. Harrop Tarn amongst the Wythburn Fells – 2.5km/1½ hours
35. By Ruthwaite and Uldale to round Over Water – 9.5km/3 hours
36. High Bowscale Tarn in the northern fells – 7km/2½ hours
37. Pooley Bridge to Heughscar Hill by way of Moor Divock – 7.5km/2½ hours
38. Patterdale to Howtown: a traverse of Ullswater's south shore – 10km/3½ hours
39. A crossing of Grisedale at the head of Ullswater – 5km/2½ hours
40. Mardale's Coffin Road from Haweswater to Swindale – 14km/5 hours

5

Hawkshead Church

THIS PRACTICAL GUIDEBOOK is a selection of my favourite low-level walks throughout the Lake District. It is an area, for those with an eye to see and a heart to perceive, whose perfection of scale and sublime beauty – of lake, tree and fell – is oft regarded as a piece of heaven fallen to earth. Whilst many will associate my writing and photography with steep places and high mountains, this book is based on a lifetime's local knowledge and love of the Lake District – Britain's largest National Park. It is designed to be inspirationally attractive, whilst at the same time harmonising map, text and photograph to provide crystal-clear practical information which is suitable to be used as a guide en route.

The routes selected vary in difficulty and length from a half-hour stroll to outings of up to five-hours' duration. More typically, they involve around two-and-a-half to three hours of leisurely walking. Sometimes level, sometimes rising to crest a low fell, mostly the walks are circular in nature, conveniently starting and finishing at the same point, providing a magnificent way to explore the many varied splendours

Windermere from Loughrigg

of the area. The length and difficulty of each walk is defined in a Fact File, and within these parameters the walks are suitable for persons of average fitness and ability, young or old.

Although a number of these walks may have never previously been described in print, I make no claims for originality. Simple observation – of the stone circles and enclosures of prehistory, of Roman forts and roads underfoot, of the Celtic and Viking place names,

the poetry of Wordsworth and the art of Beatrix Potter, the spoil of the miner and quarryman, the trod of the shepherd, the work of the Ordnance Survey, of numerous Victorian and contemporary guidebooks – provide glimpses of the many who may have trod these ways. The philosophy of my route selection is simply to offer you what I feel is the best of Lakeland walking based on my own practical experience.

Despite the generally low-level nature of most of these walks there are many potential dangers to greet the unwary. Unfenced drops, open quarry holes, mineshafts, fast-flowing streams, rivers and deep lakes can all be found throughout the region. An eye should always be kept on safety and children should be carefully

Stone circle on Burnmoor

Over Great Langdale

Gathering sheep in Buttermere

High Sweden Bridge

supervised at all times. Of course whilst one of the considerable attractions of the Lake District is the marked contrast of its four seasons, offering a variety of walking throughout the year, the walker must be adequately equipped to deal with the prevailing conditions. Similarly provision must also be made for rapidly changing weather. Wordsworth's poignant poem 'Lucy Gray' is based in fact and should be heeded:

The storm came on before its time:
She wandered up and down;
And many a hill did Lucy climb:
But never reached the town.

To keep the cost of this guidebook as low as possible without compromising quality, and to maintain a convenient and carryable size, the selection of walks has been limited to forty. There are currently two books available in this series: Book 1 and Book 2. Each book describes unique and different walks throughout the region. Together they form the most comprehensive and definitive walks' guide to the lakes and low fells of the Lake District National Park. It is the author's ambition to extend coverage of the Lake District, and also to apply the same philosophy to other areas of outstanding beauty and interest.

Walking is a lifelong ever-changing experience. It deepens your contact with nature – the earth and wind, the sounds and smells, the sun and cold, the hard and the soft – and it quickens your observation of the infinite

beauty of the natural world in harmony with man's ingenuity. In short it heightens the emotions, liberates the body, sharpens the mind and enriches the spirit. I have trod these routes many times: with my parents, alone, with friends, and currently with my young family. They are never the same; I always discover something new, and I hope to walk them in old age. Should you find such riches then I feel this guidebook will have achieved something quite remarkable.

Each walk is presented on one easy-to-view double-page spread (like a sheet of writing paper – turn the book around to read it) which includes essential information to help you easily locate and select the walk, a concise route description and clear map detailing the route. Photographs illustrate the overall nature of the area and highlight particular points of interest, so capturing the overall ambience of each walk.

WALK NUMBER
See area map on page 4 for location

WALK NAME

PREVIEW
Key locations en route

INTRODUCTION
Gives location with respect to nearest centre and provides brief descriptive 'taster'

STEP BY STEP
A balanced route description specifying key locations and highlighting points of particular interest. An alternative route may also be suggested

PHOTOGRAPHS
A variety of images have been chosen to span the seasons. While some are intended to capture the individual character of the walk by portraying the overall scenic splendour of the region, others do so by highlighting key points of interest

WALK 6   WALK 6   WALK 6   WALK 6

A CIRCUIT OF ELTER WATER BENEATH THE LANGDALES

Ullets Nest, Little Langdale, Colwith Force, Skelwith Force, Elter Water, Great Langdale

INTRODUCTION

6.5KM WEST OF AMBLESIDE. THIS CIRCUIT CONTRASTS OPEN VISTA WITH WOODED DALE, TRAVERSING THE FOOT OF THE GREAT AND LITTLE LANGDALE VALLEYS. IT ROUNDS SECRETIVE ELTER WATER, WHILST OFFERING CLASSIC VIEWS OF THE LANGDALE PIKES AND VISITING TWO DELIGHTFUL WATERFALLS.

STEP BY STEP

Follow the road and cross the bridge, continue past the Youth Hostel. In a further 100m a road branches to the right. Ascend this and keep left to make steeper ascent up the unsurfaced track. This track, delightfully wooded, is known locally as Ullets Nest and leads over the brow of the hill into Little Langdale.

Once the track levels a gate and kissing gate will be found on the left and a little path (signed Wilson Place Farm) leads across and down the fields to pass through the farmyard. Bear left along the road for 50m until a kissing gate on the right leads down Lang Parrock field to a small wooden footbridge over the River Brathay. The path continues to rise on the far side of the valley to a gate at Stang End Farm.

Bear left along the road to find High Park Farm. Go through the farm yard following the signed path into the woods. A permissive path bears off left to join the river above Colwith Force waterfall. Continue along by the banks of the river to emerge from the woods over a stile onto the

Colwith Force

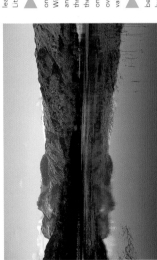

Over Elter Water to Langdale Pikes

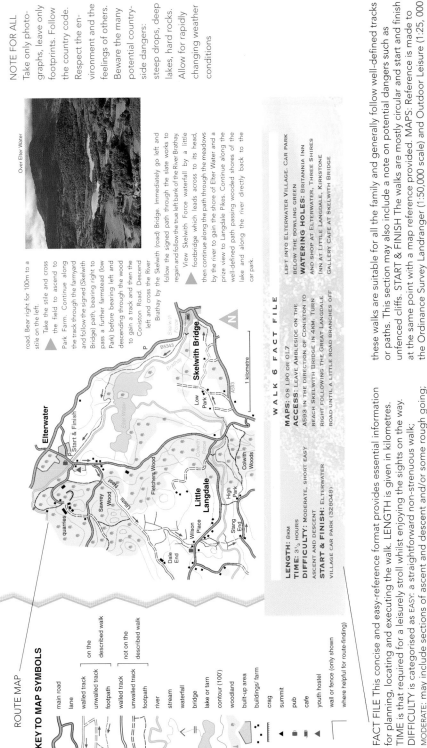

NOTE FOR ALL

Take only photographs, leave only footprints. Follow the country code. Respect the environment and the feelings of others. Beware the many potential countryside dangers: steep drops, deep lakes, hard rocks. Allow for rapidly changing weather conditions

Over Elter Water

road. Bear right for 100m to a stile on the left.

▲ Take the stile and cross the field to ascend to Park Farm. Continue along the track through the farmyard and follow the signed (Skelwith Bridge) path, bearing right to pass a further farmstead (Iow Park) before bearing left and descending through the wood to gain a track and then the Coniston Road. Descend left and cross the River Brathay.

▲ by the Skelwith (road) Bridge. Immediately go left and follow the signed path through the slate works to regain and follow the true left bank of the River Brathay. View Skelwith Force waterfall by a little footbridge which leads across to its head, then continue along the path through the meadows by the river to gain the shore of Elter Water and a prize view to Langdale Pikes. Continue along the well-defined path passing wooded shores of the lake and along the river directly back to the car park.

WALK 6 FACT FILE

LENGTH: 8KM

TIME: 3½ HOURS

DIFFICULTY: MODERATE, SHORT EASY ASCENT AND DESCENT

START & FINISH: ELTERWATER VILLAGE CAR PARK (328048)

MAPS: OS L90 OR OL7

ACCESS: LEAVE AMBLESIDE ON THE A593 IN THE DIRECTION OF CONISTON TO REACH SKELWITH BRIDGE IN 4KM. TURN RIGHT FOLLOWING THE GREAT LANGDALE ROAD UNTIL A LITTLE ROAD BRANCHES OFF

LEFT INTO ELTERWATER VILLAGE. CAR PARK BELOW THE BOWLING GREEN

WATERING HOLES: BRITANNIA INN AND SHOP AT ELTERWATER, THREE SHIRES INN AT LITTLE LANGDALE, KIRKSTONE GALLERY CAFE AT SKELWITH BRIDGE

ROUTE MAP

KEY TO MAP SYMBOLS

main road	
lane	
walled track	on the
unwalled track	described walk
footpath	
walled track	not on the
unwalled track	described walk
footpath	
river	
stream	
waterfall	
bridge	
lake or tarn	
contour (100')	
woodland	
built-up area	
buildings/ farm	
crag	
summit	
pub	
cafe	
youth hostel	
wall or fence (only shown where helpful for route-finding)	

FACT FILE This concise and easy-reference format provides essential information for planning, locating and executing the walk. LENGTH is given in kilometres. TIME is that required for a leisurely stroll whilst enjoying the sights on the way. DIFFICULTY is categorised as EASY: a straightforward non-strenuous walk; MODERATE: may include sections of ascent and descent and/or some rough going; DIFFICULT: may include strenuous ascent and descent, rough going, longevity, or require care with route-finding. NOTE: In reasonably fair summer conditions

these walks are suitable for all the family and generally follow well-defined tracks or paths. This section may also include a note on potential dangers such as unfenced cliffs. START & FINISH The walks are mostly circular and start and finish at the same point with a map reference provided. MAPS: Reference is made to the Ordnance Survey Landranger (1:50,000 scale) and Outdoor Leisure (1:25,000 scale). ACCESS is described from the nearest centre. WATERING HOLES Places for refreshment en route or those located nearby.

Cottages at Sandwick above Ullswater

The Tongue above Troutbeck Park Farm

Stanley Gill

To Lingmoor with Langdale Pikes

THE LAKE DISTRICT NATIONAL PARK is the largest in Britain, with an area of some 2,292sq km. Located at the north-west extremity of England, with the Solway Firth to the north and Scotland beyond, it is roughly circular in plan. Its 55km diameter stretches from Ravenglass on the west coast to Shap Abbey in the east, from Caldbeck in the north to Lindale and Morecambe Bay in the south. Its physical landscape is that of a mountain region, whose formative geological activity started some 500 million years ago, subsequently and dramatically shaped by the effects of glaciation.

During the last ice age, some 15,000 years ago, the movement of huge thicknesses of ice carved out a system of valleys which, roughly speaking, radiate out from the central high point of Scafell Pike, at 978m the highest mountain in England. Often likened to the spokes of a wheel these deep, narrow valleys, with their lakes, shape and define six distinctly different areas of mountains (see *Complete Lakeland Fells* by the author for details). The individual hills are known as fells, from the Viking *fjall*. From its high fells to deep valleys, by its cascading becks and great lakes, by woods, fields and craggy steeps, it is an area of immense beauty, great diversity and striking contrast.

The geology of the region is remarkably varied, and it is the rocks whose properties, soils and mineralisation have most influenced the subsequent shaping of the landscape at the hands of man. In brief, some 450 million years ago the oldest rocks of the region were laid as sedimentary deposits; these are the Skiddaw Slates which mainly shape the northern fells. Next followed a period of intense volcanic activity, uplift and mineralisation

10

which produced the core of the region – these hard rocks are known as the Borrowdale Volcanics, which typically form the Langdale Pikes. The volcanics are underlain by granite, that of Eskdale and Ennerdale. Around 420 million years ago another period of flooding produced the sedimentary Silurian Slates, and these softer rocks form the gentler, more rounded landscape of Windermere Lake and Coniston Water. The white fossilised sedimentary limestones found on the southern periphery, those of Scout Scar and Whitbarrow Scar, date from the Carboniferous period of some 300 million years ago.

To this geological skeleton add a rich botanical flora, a fine mixture of deciduous trees, and the wild of deer, squirrel, fox, golden eagle and peregrine falcon. Apply the industrious hand of man, his farms, mines and inns, his art and ingenuity, and you have a unique and fascinating landscape. Man first began to farm the landscape circa 5,000BC during the Neolithic

Prehistoric rock art in Langdale

Herdwick sheep search for winter feed in Little Langdale

The Boat House at Devoke Water

Hodge Close slate quarry

Thorneyfields Farm

Wordsworth's Dove Cottage

Slate on Castle Crag   Ice on Hunting Stile

who have probably done the most to influence the existing shape of the region. Principally farmers, it was they who named the fells and many features of the landscape. In fact we remain to this day – Birkett is of Norse origin, and my grandfather used to speak a language, which went beyond dialect, directly akin to old Norse. He found it very useful when the vicar called and failed to understand a single word! (True story.)

Two huge influences on the landscape are mineral mining, chiefly for copper and lead, and slate quarrying. Whilst mining is certainly an activity of prehistory, written record shows that the monks of Furness, circa 1150, mined haematite and manufactured iron in bloomeries sited throughout the region. Incidentally they kept their records in pencil using graphite from Seathwaite (then the only world source of the material). Reputedly the Romans worked slate, though slate quarrying increased dramatically during the industrial revolution, a period of growth which made huge demands for roofing material.

The first tourist guidebook is reputed to

period. Using stone axes manufactured from the fine-grained volcanic tuff found most notably on the Langdale Pikes, he felled the trees to clear the valleys. Recently recorded, though known and photographed by the author for many years, Neolithic man left his art in the form of rock drawings on a number of valley boulders. Most dramatically, the stone circles of Castlerigg and Swinside were also constructed during this period. Later came the Bronze Age, circa 3,000BC, and presumably the first copper mines of the Coniston fells.

The Romans, who had a profound influence on the area, arrived circa AD80 and didn't depart until early AD400. The most dramatic evidence of their occupation remains in the form of Hardknott Fort above Eskdale, Walls Castle (the highest free-standing Roman building in northern England) and the Roman roads over the great ridge of High Street and Muncaster Fell. Somewhere around AD900 the Vikings arrived and it is they region's best interests to heart. These of course include the National Park Authority and the National Trust, both of whom are ably assisted by energetic bands of volunteers who generously give their time to support the professionals. Other protective organisations include the Friends of the Lake District and the Cumbria Broadleaves partnership.

One of the great joys of the Lake District is its freedom of access. Above the fell wall this is generally unrestricted, and below in the dales and through the fields there exists a comprehensive system of rights of way – fully utilised by this book. Whatever the weather, throughout the seasons the Lake District's stone-built farms and cottages, wild fells, enchanting woods, dashing waterfalls, lakes and tarns and welcoming inns present an ever-changing kaleidoscope of mood and colour. It really is one of the most special places on earth.

Bowscale Tarn

Wasdale Church

Stickle Tarn

be that of Father West in 1778, and the appreciation of the beauty of the Lake District took off in earnest from then on. The Romantic poets of the early 1800s consolidated the position, notably under the influence of William Wordsworth, who also produced a best-selling guidebook to the area. Later, twentieth-century influences included Beatrix Potter with her 'Peter Rabbit' books and Hugh Walpole's 'Rogue Herries' novels.

The Lake District officially became a National Park in the 1950s. Today a number of organised bodies have the

AMBLESIDE'S HIGH TO LOW SWEDEN BRIDGE

Sweden Bridge Lane to Scandale Pass, High Sweden Bridge, Low Sweden Bridge, Nook Lane

Sweden Lane

INTRODUCTION

AMBLESIDE, TUMBLING STEEPLY THROUGH WOODED GORGE AND OVER ROCKY FALL, SCANDALE BECK IS CROSSED BY TWO STONE-ARCH BRIDGES. THIS CIRCUIT CROSSES THE TWO SWEDEN BRIDGES, FIRST RISING BETWEEN STONE WALLS AND ENCLOSING WOODS BEFORE MAKING OPEN DESCENT WITH WONDERFUL VIEWS OVER LAKE AND FELL.

INTRODUCTION

STEP BY STEP

▲ Opposite the car park the Kirkstone Pass road rises steeply out of Ambleside. Follow this until, some 100m past the Golden Rule Inn, Sweden Bridge lane cuts off left.

▲ Rise with the lane without deviation until the surfacing ends at a wooden gate. Continue between stone walls over rough stone and occasional cobbling up the old packhorse lane which leads to Scandale Pass. As the track falls slightly to overlook the gorge of Scandale Beck a gate leads into the mixed birch, hazel, oak and ash of Rough Sides Wood.

▲ The track continues to rise past old slate quarries until a lesser track cuts off left to cross the beck by the ancient flattened stone arch of High Sweden Bridge. Note the name Sweden which comes from the Viking *Svioinn* meaning 'moorland cleared by burning.'

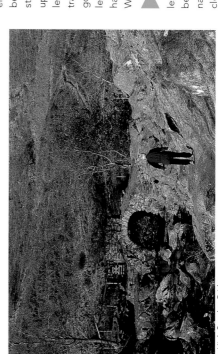

To High Sweden Bridge

14

▲ Rise with the path to intercept a better-defined track leading back left down the hillside through the gap in the stone wall marked by a ladder stile.

▲ The open track, with breathtaking views over Loughrigg to the Coniston and Langdale fells and over Rydal Water and Windermere Lake, leads down to Low Sweden Bridge. Cross to gain the end of Nook Lane by Nook End Farm. The lane leads back to the Kirkstone Pass road just below the Golden Rule Inn.

Looking to Rydal Water from near Low Sweden Bridge

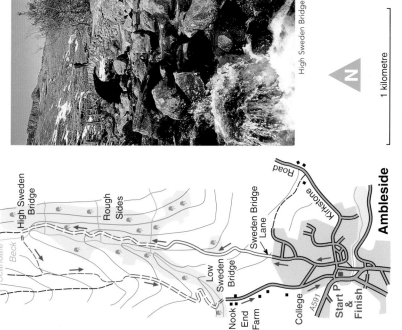

High Sweden Bridge

N

1 kilometre

Scandale Beck

High Sweden Bridge

Rough Sides

Low Sweden Bridge

Sweden Bridge Lane

Kirkstone Road

Nook End Farm

College

A591

Start P & Finish

Ambleside

WALK 1 FACT FILE

START & FINISH: AMBLESIDE CENTRAL CAR PARK (375047)

MAPS: OS L90 OR OL7

ACCESS: AMBLESIDE'S MAIN CAR PARK IS FOUND JUST THROUGH THE CENTRE BY THE SIDE OF A591 RYDAL ROAD TO KESWICK

WATERING HOLES: THE GOLDEN RULE INN

LENGTH: 5KM

TIME: 1¾ HOURS

DIFFICULTY: EASY GOING WITH GRADUAL ASCENT AND DESCENT

LOUGHRIGG'S LILY TARN ABOVE AMBLESIDE

Bridge House, Rothay Park, Miller Bridge, Loughrigg Fell, Lily Tarn

INTRODUCTION

AMBLESIDE. OCCUPYING A SUBLIME POSITION, LOUGHRIGG IS THE DELIGHTFUL LOW FELL WHICH RUNS FROM AMBLESIDE AND THE HEAD OF WINDERMERE LAKE, TOWARDS BOTH LANGDALE AND GRASMERE. THIS CIRCUIT CROSSES THE RIVER ROTHAY BY MILLER BRIDGE AND RISES TO A CRAGGY VIEWPOINT BEFORE TRAVERSING BY LITTLE LILY TARN TO RETURN VIA THE STONE LANE OF MILLER BROW.

INTRODUCTION

Lily Tarn

STEP BY STEP

▶ Take the wooden footbridge from the car cark and go right to pass the water wheel and Bridge House. Bear right along Compston Road and continue until, at the next junction (cinema on corner) Vicarage Road joins the side road and leads to Rothay Park. Follow the main path through the park to emerge by a flat bridge over Stockghyll Beck, immediately followed by the stone-arched Miller Bridge over the River Rothay.

▶ Cross this and bear right along the road over the cattle grid until in a few metres a steep surfaced road rises to the left. Climb the track which becomes unsurfaced by the buildings of Brow Head. At the S-bend beyond, a stone stile leads up and off left.

▶ The path squeezes through a stone stile before rising up the open hillside above. A variety of routes is possible, though for the best views over Windermere Lake it is best to keep left before rising to the first little rocky knoll. A higher rocky knoll follows (definitive views of the Fairfield Horseshoe to the north).

Miller Bridge

16

Beyond this the way drops right to a well-defined path. Follow the path to pass a little pond before cresting a rise and dropping to the lovely little pocket handkerchief of Lily Tarn (flowers bloom late June to July). The path skirts the right edge of the tarn to roughly follow the broad crest of Loughrigg Fell. A gate/stile leads to the base of a further knoll and this is ascended to another worthy viewpoint. Take the path erring right in descent to find a track below. (The main summit can be gained by following

the middle path left rising along the fell for a further 1.5 km).

▲ Bear right to a gate which leads through the stone wall perimeter and into a field. Continue descending the track to intercept the original route just above the buildings of Brow Head. After recrossing Miller Bridge bear left to follow the track by the side of Stockghyll Beck. Bear right by the main Rydal Road to find the car park just beyond the Fire Station.

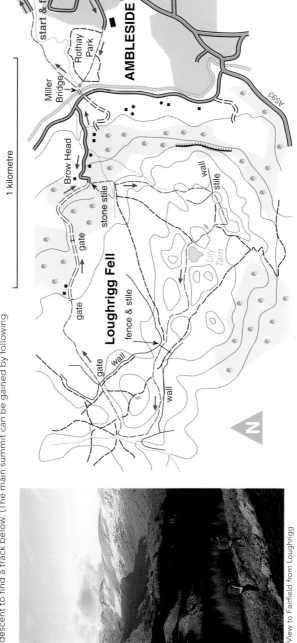

View to Fairfield from Loughrigg

WALK 2 FACT FILE

LENGTH: 5KM

TIME: 1³⁄₄ HOURS

DIFFICULTY: MODERATE, WITH STRAIGHTFORWARD ASCENT AND DESCENT

START & FINISH: AMBLESIDE CENTRAL CAR PARK (375047)

MAPS: OS L90 OR OL7

ACCESS: AMBLESIDE'S MAIN CAR PARK IS

FOUND JUST THROUGH THE CENTRE BY THE SIDE OF A591 RYDAL ROAD TO KESWICK

WATERING HOLES: CAFES AND INNS ABOUND IN AMBLESIDE

THE ROUND OF RYDAL WATER

Rydal Water, Loughrigg Terrace, Rydal Cave, Rydal Mount, Coffin Road, White Moss Common Fell

INTRODUCTION

3KM WEST OF AMBLESIDE. NESTLING DEEP BETWEEN THE FELLS RYDAL WATER LIES AT THE HEART OF WORDSWORTH COUNTRY. THIS WALK PASSES HIS FORMER HOUSE TO TRAVERSE THROUGH ONE OF ENGLAND'S MOST SUBLIME LANDSCAPES OF WOODS AND FELL, FINALLY OFFERING UNPARALLELED VIEWS OVER BOTH RYDAL WATER AND GRASMERE LAKE.

By Rydal Cave

STEP BY STEP

▲ From either car park walk to gain the banks of the River Rothay. Take the wooden footbridge and continue straight on, taking the path that leads through the woods away from the river. A kissing gate emerges from the woods onto a stony track. (An alternative route bears left to traverse by the shoreline of Rydal Water.) Take the path above, ascending the hillside through the bracken to gain a level path known as Loughrigg Terrace. Traverse left along the Terrace path until the entrance to Rydal Cave is encountered - old slate quarry.

▲ Descend and pass a further quarry until the track descends to a gate above the shore of Rydal Water. Go down to gain a low path just above the shoreline of Rydal Water. This serves an iron gate which leads into delightful oak woods. Continue along to cross the river, flowing from the lake, by a narrow wooden footbridge.

Over Rydal Water to Nab Scar

18

Bear right along the road until in 100m the lane on the left is ascended. This passes Rydal Mount, the final home of William Wordsworth, to find a track traversing left above the house. This is the old Coffin Road between Ambleside and Grasmere. Follow this, scenically traversing across the hillside through woods and open spaces for 1.8km, until the point it becomes surfaced, with a little pond to the right and with a stony track descending to the left (leading directly back to White Moss Common car park). Follow a grassy path which rises to the left up the hillside.

Soon the path levels (exposed craggy drop) before continuing to gain the high point of the fell. Unparalleled views over both Grasmere Lake and Rydal Water. After first moving in the direction of Rydal Water a little care will find a path descending the shoulder of the hillside to gain, in 150m, a narrow surfaced road. Bear left descending this to regain White Moss Common (by the ice-cream van).

Down White Moss Common

WALK 3 FACT FILE

START & FINISH: WHITE MOSS COMMON CAR PARKS (348066)

ACCESS: LEAVE AMBLESIDE ON THE A591 IN THE DIRECTION OF GRASMERE TO FIND WHITE MOSS COMMON IN 3KM

LENGTH: 6KM

TIME: 2½ HOURS

DIFFICULTY: MODERATE, SLIGHT ASCENT AND DESCENT

MAPS: OS L90 OR OL7

NATIONAL TRUST CAR PARKS LOCATED ON EITHER SIDE OF THE ROAD

WATERING HOLES: FRED PERRUZA ICE-CREAM VAN AT WHITE MOSS COMMON, BADGER BAR AT RYDAL

1 kilometre

N

White Moss Common Fell

Start & Finish

Baneriggs

Grasmere

Loughrigg Terrace

Rydal Water

Coffin Road

Nab Scar

Rydal Caves

Rydal Mount

Rydal

Pelter Bridge

A591

TO ALCOCK TARN ABOVE GRASMERE

Dove Cottage, Duck Pond, Butter Crags, Alcock Tarn, Greenhead Gill

Dove Cottage, Wordsworth's former home

INTRODUCTION

GRASMERE. HIGH ABOVE GRASMERE, HIDDEN WITHIN A FOLD OF HERON PIKE, NESTLES ALCOCK TARN. OFFERING UNRIVALLED VIEWS OVER THE VALE OF GRASMERE THIS ROUTE ASCENDS THROUGH THE TREES OF WOOD CLOSE AND THEN THE OPEN FELL ROUNDING BUTTER CRAGS TO OVERLOOK LITTLE ALCOCK TARN BEFORE DESCENDING THE ZIGZAGS TO GREENHEAD GILL.

INTRODUCTION

STEP BY STEP

▲ Head out of the village to cross the main road and bear left through Town End, to pass by Wordsworth's famous former home, Dove Cottage. Continue up the lane to pass a duck pond (badly overgrown) opposite How Top Farm. Bear left at the junction and climb the steep hill until in a further 180m an unsurfaced track (signed Alcock Tarn) bears off to the left.

▲ Rise to a gate and enter the mixed beech woods of Wood Close. The track continues to rise, passing a little man-made pond before moving out onto open fell. Through a little gate in the stone wall, rise again to cross the little beck over a tiny stone-arch bridge (the smallest in Lakeland?). Contour around beneath the rocky knoll of Butter Crags (wrongly labelled Grey Crag by the OS) and ascend to the grassy shoulder. Breathtaking views extend over the Vale of Grasmere, particularly from the top of Butter Crags. Cross through a gap in the stone wall to overlook Alcock Tarn, which seems of plain aspect when compared with the loveliness below – how could it be other?

Alcock Tarn with Great Rigg rising beyond

The distinctive peak of Great Rigg rises high above. Traverse left by the tarn and follow the path which leads down to make steep descent of the zigzags. Keeping above the forestry wall descend to the edge of Greenhead Gill and follow down this until it can be crossed by a little wooden footbridge. A surfaced track leads through trees and by houses to emerge into the open by a quiet road. Bear first left then right to arrive at the Swan Inn by the side of the main A591. Go left to find a crossing point, cross the road, then go left until the second signed footpath heads right, across the fields back to Stock Lane. The path is well signed, though muddy in wet weather, and leads first to the banks of the River Rothay then passes converted cottages, once THE WORKMAN'S READING ROOM, to finally pass Grasmere School and exit onto Stock Lane.

Over Grasmere Lake to Butter Crags

To Alcock Tarn via tiny stone arch

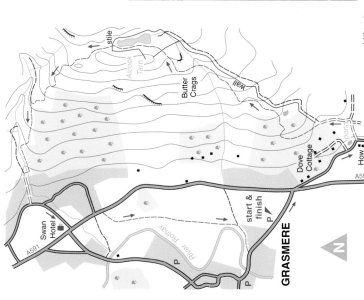

1 kilometre

GRASMERE

WALK 4 FACT FILE

LENGTH: 5KM

TIME: 2 HOURS

DIFFICULTY: MODERATE, WITH MILDLY STRENUOUS ASCENT AND DESCENT

START & FINISH: GRASMERE, STOCK LANE CAR PARK (328048)

MAPS: OS L90 OR OL7

ACCESS: GRASMERE CAN BE FOUND NORTH OF AMBLESIDE SOME 6KM ALONG THE A591 TOWARDS KESWICK. STOCK LANE LEADS DIRECTLY OFF THE MAIN ROAD INTO THE VILLAGE

WATERING HOLES: THE SWAN INN

HIGH CLOSE AND HUNTING STILE ABOVE LANGDALE AND GRASMERE

High Close, Dow Bank Shooting Butts, Wyke Woods, Hunting Stile, Redbank Wood

Shooting butts on Hunting Stile

INTRODUCTION

6KM WEST OF AMBLESIDE. A PLEASANT ROUND COMBINING OPEN FELLSIDE AND SLOPES OF MIXED WOODLAND WITH DELIGHTFUL POSITION OVER BOTH GRASMERE AND GREAT LANGDALE. FROM THE HIGH POINT OF THE GRASMERE TO ELTERWATER ROAD THIS ROUTE STRIKES WEST ALONG THE HUNTINGSTILE SHOULDER BEFORE DESCENDING TOWARDS GRASMERE BY WYKE WOOD AND REASCENDING BY THE SIDE OF REDBANK WOOD.

STEP BY STEP

▲ From the little rock face above the road follow the grassy path around onto the open fellside. The route crosses the deep dip, a natural little valley rift which crosses over the shoulder of the fell, then climbs steeply up the end of Huntingstile Crag. Pass through the rocky knolls by a tiny tarnlet to gain a higher cairned height. Descend and continue along the shoulder until, at a point below the larger knoll of Dow Bank the path contours around to the right. Follow this then bear left to pass the roofless remains and flat firing area of the old shooting butts, last used by Langdale and Grasmere volunteers in the 1940s and known locally as 'The Targets'.

▲ Continue, to intercept the path coming over the top of Spedding Crag. Bear right in descent. The path passes through the juniper, by two level shooting areas, to find a gate in the wall on the edge of Wyke Plantation. A path leads down through mixed woods to swing left and follow above the stream with a wall to the right. An old iron kissing gate leads onto a surfaced driveway. Bear left down the driveway to the road (the obvious direct route to the road bears a sign 'Private Road').

▲ Swing right and follow the road for 400m until, opposite a red post box in the wall of Lea Cottage, a surfaced lane ascends to the right.

Frozen tarn on Hunting Stile, Fairfield forms the backdrop

22

Follow the lane, past Hunting Stile Lodge, to continue over cobbles.

▲ At its head the middle high gate leads to open ground. Continue by the wall, with Redbank Wood to the left, to follow above the little valley which cuts down from the heights, and on to a gate in the wall to regain the boggy dip in the shoulder just below the point at which the original path climbs Huntingstile Crag.

Over High Close to Hunting Stile

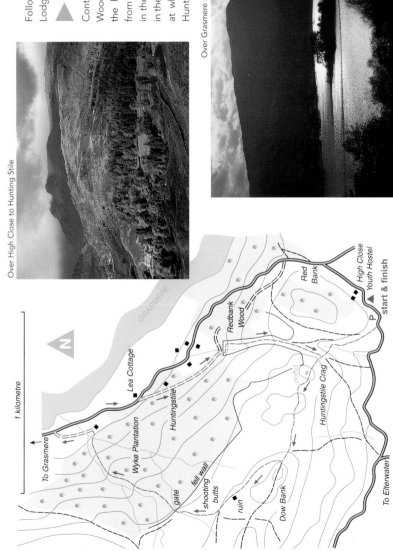

Over Grasmere Lake, shoulder of Hunting Stile to left

WALK 5 FACT FILE

LENGTH: 4KM

TIME: 1½ HOURS

DIFFICULTY: MODERATE, WITH MILDLY STRENUOUS ASCENT AND DESCENT

START & FINISH: HIGH CLOSE, A LITTLE ROADSIDE PARKING SPACE ON THE LANGDALE SIDE (338052)

MAPS: OS L90 OR OL7

ACCESS: APPROACH EITHER BY RED BANK (NARROW AND STEEP) ABOVE GRASMERE OR REACHED IN 6KM FROM AMBLESIDE BY A VARIETY OF ROADS ABOVE SKELWITH BRIDGE/LANGDALE

WATERING HOLES: NONE EN ROUTE

A CIRCUIT OF ELTER WATER BENEATH THE LANGDALES

Ullets Nest, Little Langdale, Colwith Force, Skelwith Force, Elter Water, Great Langdale

INTRODUCTION

6.5KM WEST OF AMBLESIDE. THIS CIRCUIT CONTRASTS OPEN VISTA WITH WOODED DALE, TRAVERSING THE FOOT OF THE GREAT AND LITTLE LANGDALE VALLEYS. IT ROUNDS SECRETIVE ELTER WATER, WHILST OFFERING CLASSIC VIEWS OF THE LANGDALE PIKES AND VISITING TWO DELIGHTFUL WATERFALLS.

Colwith Force

STEP BY STEP

▲ Follow the road and cross the bridge, continue past the Youth Hostel. In a further 100m a road branches to the right. Ascend this and keep left to make steeper ascent up the unsurfaced track. This track, delightfully wooded, is known locally as Ullets Nest and leads over the brow of the hill into Little Langdale.

▲ Once the track levels a gate and kissing gate will be found on the left and a little path (signed Wilson Place Farm) leads across and down the fields to pass through the farmyard. Bear left along the road for 50m until a kissing gate on the right leads down Lang Parrock field to a small wooden footbridge over the River Brathay. The path continues to rise on the far side of the valley to a gate at Stang End Farm.

▲ Bear left along the road to find High Park Farm. Go through the farm yard following the signed path into the woods. A permissive path bears off left to join the river above Colwith Force waterfall. Continue along by the banks of the river to emerge from the woods over a stile onto the

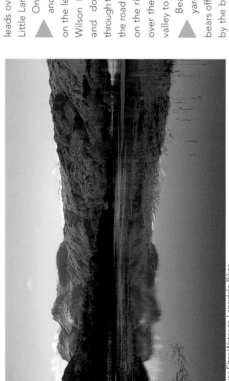

Over Elter Water to Langdale Pikes

Over Elter Water

road. Bear right for 100m to a stile on the left.

▲ Take the stile and cross the field to ascend to Park Farm. Continue along the track through the farmyard and follow the signed (Skelwith Bridge) path, bearing right to pass a further farmstead (low Park) before bearing left and descending through the wood to gain a track and then the Coniston Road. Descend left and cross the River Brathay by the Skelwith (road) Bridge. Immediately go left and follow the signed path through the slate works to regain and follow the true left bank of the River Brathay.

▲ View Skelwith Force waterfall by a little footbridge which leads across to its head, then continue along the path through the meadows by the river to gain the shore of Elter Water and a prize view to Langdale Pikes. Continue along the well-defined path passing wooded shores of the lake and along the river directly back to the car park.

WALK 6 FACT FILE

LENGTH: 8KM

TIME: 3½ HOURS

DIFFICULTY: MODERATE, SHORT EASY ASCENT AND DESCENT

START & FINISH: ELTERWATER VILLAGE CAR PARK (328048)

MAPS: OS L90 OR OL7

ACCESS: LEAVE AMBLESIDE ON THE A593 IN THE DIRECTION OF CONISTON TO REACH SKELWITH BRIDGE IN 4KM. TURN RIGHT FOLLOWING THE GREAT LANGDALE ROAD UNTIL A LITTLE ROAD BRANCHES OFF LEFT INTO ELTERWATER VILLAGE. CAR PARK BELOW THE BOWLING GREEN

WATERING HOLES: BRITANNIA INN AND SHOP AT ELTERWATER, THREE SHIRES INN AT LITTLE LANGDALE, KIRKSTONE GALLERY CAFE AT SKELWITH BRIDGE

LINGMOOR FELL FROM CHAPEL STILE

Elterwater Quarry, Baysbrown Wood, Bield Crag Cairn, Brown How – Lingmoor Fell, Banks Quarry

INTRODUCTION

7KM WEST OF AMBLESIDE. AN EVOCATIVE NAME FOR THE LOVELY HEATHER-CLAD FELL WHICH SEPARATES THE LANGDALES. UTILISING A NETWORK OF QUARRY-MEN'S TRACKS THIS ROUTE FIRST ASCENDS LINGMOOR FROM LITTLE LANGDALE THEN TRAVERSES THE SPINE, RETURNING TO DESCEND THE GREAT LANGDALE SLOPES DIRECTLY TO CHAPEL STILE.

On Lingmoor above Little Langdale

STEP BY STEP

▲ A little gate leads to the wooden footbridge crossing Great Langdale Beck. Bear right beyond the bridge and briefly follow by the river to gain the track leading beneath the masonry banks of Elterwater Quarry. Climb the track to gain the quarry road and bear right between the sheds/buildings of this working slate quarry. Bear left to leave the quarry and follow a track which gains a surfaced road by Crossgates House.

▲ Opposite the house a path climbs steeply up the wooded hillside of Baysbrown Wood. Follow the path up through the wood before dropping down to gain the larger track of Ullets Nest which leads into Little Langdale. Go right to immediately pass through a gate and ascend the track. It levels and continues to make a final rise around a little knoll – the highest point of the track. After a further 200m a gate on the right leads out onto the fellside (before Dale End Farm).

Lingmoor, above Little Langdale Tarn

26

Follow the path which winds its way up the Little Langdale flank of Lingmoor. As the shoulder is crested it is worth crossing left to the Bield Crag Cairn for a fine open view.

▲ Cross to the centre of the shoulder to take the grassy track which rises steeply near the crest of the fell. (Note the stile leading through the stone wall, situated on the col roughly opposite Bield Crag Cairn – this will be taken in descent.) A stone wall runs along the crest to the right. Finally a steeper section of ascent climbs to cross the fence by a cairn, and gains the summit of Lingmoor – Brown How. Exalted position looking over Little Langdale to the southern fells and over Lingmoor Tarn to the Langdale Pikes.

▲ Make return by the same route to find the stile through the stone wall. Cross the stile, descending the grassy path to gain a track which leads right down to the abandoned slate level of Banks Quarry. Continue into Baysbrown Wood to intercept in a short way the path taken in ascent.

Lingmoor Spine

WALK 7 FACT FILE

START & FINISH: CHAPEL STILE, LIMITED VERGE PARKING WITHIN THE PERIMETER OF THE VILLAGE (323052)

MAPS: OS L90 OR OL7

ACCESS: LEAVE AMBLESIDE ON THE A593 IN THE DIRECTION OF CONISTON TO REACH SKELWITH BRIDGE IN 4KM. TURN RIGHT AND FOLLOW THE GREAT LANGDALE ROAD TO CHAPEL STILE

WATERING HOLES: WAINWRIGHT'S INN, CAFE AT THE VILLAGE CO-OP

LENGTH: 7KM

TIME: 2½ HOURS

DIFFICULTY: DIFFICULT, GENERALLY ON GOOD TRACKS THOUGH BOGGY IN PLACES WITH RELATIVELY STRENUOUS ASCENT AND DESCENT

STICKLE TARN DESCENDING BY HORSE INTAKE AND MILL GILL

Stickle Ghyll Waterfalls, Stickle Tarn Dam, Pavey Ark, Horse Intake, Mill Gill

Stickle Ghyll, Langdale

INTRODUCTION

10.5KM WEST OF AMBLESIDE. FED BY BRIGHT BECK, STICKLE TARN OCCUPIES A LITTLE MOUNTAIN SANCTUARY BELOW THE GREAT CLIFF OF PAVEY ARK. THIS ROUTE TAKES THE POPULAR PATH RISING BY STICKLE GHYLL TO THE DAM BEFORE SKIRTING ITS EDGE TO DESCEND BY THE PLEASANT GRASSY TRACKWAY LEADING THROUGH HORSE INTAKE ABOVE THE RAVINE OF MILL GILL.

STEP BY STEP

▲ Leave the head of the car park to locate the rough stone-cobbled track which follows up the west bank of Stickle Ghyll Beck. After 600m cross the wooden footbridge and continue steeply up the east bank of the Ghyll, passing above the splendid waterfalls. Continue until Pavey Ark launches into view above the mountain tarn. To visit the dam wade, or find suitable stepping stones to cross the shallow masonry-cobbled overflow. Return, to follow an anticlockwise direction around the tarn until at a point just before a small feeder beck, a path splits off to the right. Go right and ascend with the path for 300m until a slight recess in the flank of the grassy hillside leads gently up right to a level boggy shoulder away from the main path (which continues to gain the heights of Blea Rigg).

▲ The faintly discernible (at the time of writing) path strengthens beyond the col to form a definite track which leads down towards the walled enclosure of Horse Intake. Quit the main grassy track to go left through a narrow gap in the stone wall of the Intake. The path leads diagonally down through the Intake, to cross a stream before making a boggy exit through a gap in the bottom stone wall. Bear left to find a well

Pavey Ark above Stickle Tarn

defined path just above the head of the ravine of Mill Gill.

Follow the path, making winding descent away from Mill Gill. Intercept a stone path which falls, beneath a small crag with holly tree, diagonally left down the hillside to regain the banks of Mill Gill above the stone walls. Cross Mill Gill Beck via the little stone-slab bridge and take the gate leading to a walled lane which falls to the back of Millbeck Farm.

Bear right through the wooden gate and cross the beck by stone slabs immediately below the large yew tree. The path leads to a wooden footbridge, crossing Stickle Ghyll Beck, and a little gate beyond leads to the surfaced access road. Turn right to regain the car park by crossing in front of the Stickle Barn.

Ice on Stickle Tarn

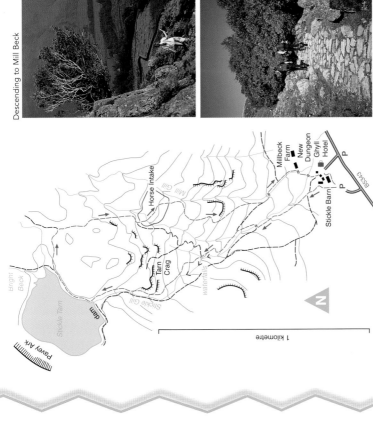
Descending to Mill Beck

To Stickle Ghyll

1 kilometre

WALK 8 FACT FILE

CAR PARK NEAR NEW DUNGEON GHYLL (295064)

MAPS: OS L90 OR OL6

ACCESS: LEAVE AMBLESIDE ON THE A593 IN THE DIRECTION OF CONISTON TO REACH SKELWITH BRIDGE IN 4KM. TURN RIGHT AND FOLLOW THE GREAT LANGDALE ROAD TO PASS THE NEW DUNGEON GHYLL HOTEL. FIND EXTENSIVE CAR PARK ON RIGHT

WATERING HOLES: STICKLE BARN AND NEW DUNGEON GHYLL HOTEL

LENGTH: 3.5KM

TIME: 2 HOURS

DIFFICULTY: DIFFICULT, WITH RELATIVELY STRENUOUS ASCENT THOUGH EASIER IN DESCENT

START & FINISH: NATIONAL TRUST

OVER HOLME FELL BY HODGE CLOSE AND YEW TREE TARN

Hodge Close Quarry, High Oxen Fell, High Cross, Yew Tree Tarn, Holme Ground Reservoirs

Climber on Hodge Close Quarry

STEP BY STEP

▲ Beware: the quarry hole is unfenced in places and its walls are sheer. Now unworked it serves as an adventure playground for climbers and divers. Go round the southern end of the great hole to find a little track and a path/lesser track which leads off left.

▲ This track keeps right of the boundary fence to pass the first hole and the next (which is called Parrock Quarry) on their east flank. Emerge onto an unsurfaced lane by a 'duckpond' and bear right to pass through High Oxen Fell Farm. Keep right along the now-surfaced lane to emerge by side of the main Ambleside to Coniston road at High Cross. A footpath will be found to the right of the road.

▲ Cross the stile and follow the path. At a point a little way above Yew Tree Tarn the path veers right to follow along above the little feeder beck. The large rectangular basin on the left used to be a trout hatchery.

Yew Tree Tarn

Bear right by the footbridge to pass through the tall elegant fir-tree plantation and continue through a gap in the stone wall before bearing left along a rough path through the mixed deciduous trees of Harry Guards Wood. At a point just before the level path passes between two great boulders, another path rises to the right.

 Ascend this, rising by Uskdale Gap to pass over the notched crest of Holme Fell. Descend the fellside to the head of the largest little reservoir. Both sides are boggy though it may be most interesting to pass on the left (west) side. Cross the slate-slab outfall bridge and continue right following the path over a little col and down to a grassy track. Descend the track to intercept a stony lane and bear right to follow this back to the end of Hodge Close Quarry.

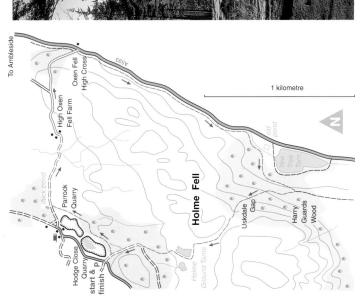

Fir above Yew Tree Tarn

WALK 9 FACT FILE

LENGTH: 5KM

TIME: 2½ HOURS

DIFFICULTY: DIFFICULT, WITH MODERATELY STRENUOUS ROUGH AND BOGGY GOING OVER HOLME FELL

START & FINISH: HODGE CLOSE QUARRY BANK (316017)

MAPS: OS L90 OR OL7

ACCESS: LEAVE AMBLESIDE ON THE A593 IN THE DIRECTION OF CONISTON TO PASS YEW TREE TARN AND YEW TREE AND HIGH YEW TREE FARMS. TAKE THE FIRST ROAD LEADING OFF TO THE RIGHT (FOUND 2.5KM NORTH OF CONISTON). FOLLOW THE NARROW ROAD UNTIL IT DESCENDS TO OPEN ONTO AN EXPANSIVE EMBANKMENT OF SLATE WASTE

WATERING HOLES: TEAS AT THE OLD FORGE IN THE HAMLET OF HODGE CLOSE

WRAY CASTLE BY THE SHORES OF WINDERMERE LAKE

Pinstones Point, Wood Close Point, High Wray Bay, Watbarrow Point, Low Wray Bay, Wray Castle

INTRODUCTION

8KM SOUTH OF AMBLESIDE. A LOVELY MAINLY LEVEL WOODED WALK EXPLORING THE INTRICACIES OF THE WEST SHORE OF WINDERMERE LAKE. A TRACK LEADS TO HIGH WRAY BAY FROM WHERE A PATH CONTINUES THROUGH THE WOODS AND OUT TO WATBARROW POINT BEFORE CLIMBING TO ROUND WRAY CASTLE AND CHURCH.

Wray Church

STEP BY STEP

▲ Head north from the car park to follow the level wooded track above the lakeshore. Pleasant woods and lovely views across the lake will be greatly enhanced by the quiet which will return should the speedboat ban come into force. Round Wood Close Point to pass a boat house and High Wray Bay (a portion of which is portioned off for public swimming).

▲ As the bridleway begins to leave the water's edge a gate off right leads to a path. Follow the path, pass a further boathouse near Epley Point, to continue by the lake shore until the path rises to enter the woods. A hill is crested and descent made towards the lake. At the bottom of the wood a way right can be made out onto the rocky promontory of Watbarrow Point with a fine view up the lake. Return to the main path and continue to a boathouse by Low Wray Bay.

▲ Bear left and ascend by the edge of the wood with open fields and increasingly fine aspect to the right. Keep right to emerge

View to Lake Windermere from Wray Castle

32

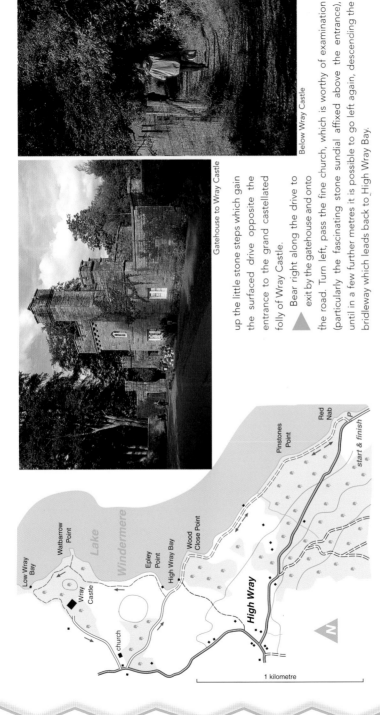

Gatehouse to Wray Castle

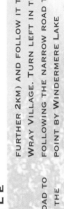

Below Wray Castle

up the little stone steps which gain the surfaced drive opposite the entrance to the grand castellated folly of Wray Castle.

▲ Bear right along the drive to exit by the gatehouse and onto the road. Turn left, pass the fine church, which is worthy of examination (particularly the fascinating stone sundial affixed above the entrance), until in a few further metres it is possible to go left again, descending the bridleway which leads back to High Wray Bay.

WALK 10 FACT FILE

LENGTH: 5.5KM

TIME: 2 HOURS

DIFFICULTY: EASY, ON GOOD TRACKS AND PATHS WITH SLIGHT ASCENT AND DESCENT TO ROUND WRAY CASTLE

START & FINISH: RED NAB CAR PARK (385995)

MAPS: OS L90/96 OR OL7

ACCESS: TAKE A593 CONISTON ROAD TO TURN LEFT AT CLAPPERSGATE ALONG THE B5286 HAWKSHEAD ROAD. TAKE THE FIRST MINOR ROAD OFF TO THE LEFT (IN A FURTHER 2KM) AND FOLLOW IT TO HIGH WRAY VILLAGE. TURN LEFT IN THE VILLAGE FOLLOWING THE NARROW ROAD TO RED NAB POINT BY WINDERMERE LAKE

WATERING HOLES: NONE EN ROUTE

HAWKSHEAD HEIGHTS

Old Grammar School, Church, Roger Ground, Howe Farm, Guinea Hill, Hawkshead Moor

INTRODUCTION

8KM SOUTH-WEST OF AMBLESIDE. HAWKSHEAD'S OLD GRAMMAR SCHOOL AND PARISH CHURCH LEAD TO A ROUTE ABOVE ESTHWAITE WATER, WHICH EXPLORES THE PEACEFUL SOLITUDE OF MIXED WOODLAND AND GAINS EXPANSIVE VIEWS FROM HAWKSHEAD MOOR DESPITE RECENT AFFORESTATION. THIS ANTICLOCKWISE CIRCUIT RISES FROM HAWKSHEAD TO EXPLORE ITS WESTERN HEIGHTS.

Stone flag fence above Hawkshead Church

STEP BY STEP

▲ The old Grammar School will be found opposite the car park. Pass the school, little changed since young Wordsworth carved his name and wrote his first poetry in the 1780s. Go through the iron gate to enter the churchyard. St Michael's Parish Church is sited in a wonderfully elevated position above the village, with views already extending to the high fells beyond. Leave by an iron gate and keep along the path. The upright slate-stone flags used to form the boundary fence on the right are a common feature hereabouts. Bear left at the junction and follow across fields until a little lane emerges onto the surfaced road at Roger Ground.

▲ Go right, then left onto the lane which leads to Howe Farm. Pass by to the left of the tarn and descend the drive to the surfaced road above Esthwaite Water. Turn right. Bear right again in a further 300m. Follow through the buildings to make an

Hawkshead Moor

exit left, crossing a bridge over the beck.

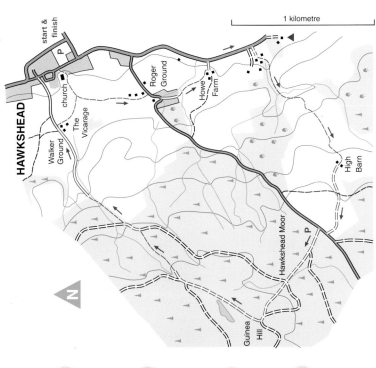

▲ Rise up the muddy leafy lane, with a deepening ravine to the right, to a stile. Bear left across the field, marker posts, to rise up and follow the path and track to pass between the buildings of High Barn. Continue to gain the road. Bear right, then left to pass the car park and enter Moor Top Forest, née Hawkshead Moor.

▲ Keep straight along the track, without deviation at the 3-way junction, rising to find the track splitting near the top of the rise. (A short diversion left to ascend the cleared Guinea Hill will reveal views to the west coast and Pennine Hills.)

▲ Go right ascending the lesser track which undulates to pass a tarn (hidden in the trees) before falling to intercept another track. Bear right at the junction and descend the track to another junction. Keep left along this new track for only a few metres until a path cuts right, down the edge of the forestry. Join a lane to bear right (junction) just below some cottages and pass by the entrance to The Vicarage before rejoining the original route just above the church.

Over Esthwaite Water to Hawkshead Moor

HAWKSHEAD
start & finish
P
church
The Vicarage
Walker Ground
Roger Ground
Howe Farm
Hawkshead Moor
Guinea Hill
High Barn
P

1 kilometre

N

WALK 11 FACT FILE

LENGTH: 6KM

TIME: 2 HOURS

DIFFICULTY: MODERATE, GENERALLY ON GOOD TRACKS OR PATHS WITH MILDLY STRENUOUS ASCENT

START & FINISH: HAWKSHEAD CAR PARK (355981)

MAPS: OS L90 OR OL7

ACCESS: FROM AMBLESIDE FOLLOW THE A593 CONISTON ROAD TO TURN LEFT AT CLAPPERSGATE AND FOLLOW THE B5286 TO HAWKSHEAD

WATERING HOLES: TEEMING IN THE VILLAGE

TO CLAIFE HEIGHTS FROM FAR SAWREY

Moss Eccles Tarn, Wise Een Tarn, Claife Heights, High Blind How, High & Low Pate Crags

INTRODUCTION

12KM SOUTH OF AMBLESIDE. DISCOVERING THE SECRETIVE HEIGHTS BETWEEN WINDERMERE LAKE AND THE VALE OF HAWKSHEAD THIS WALK IS PACKED WITH INTEREST, REVEALING HIDDEN TARNS AND AN ARRAY OF BREATHTAKING VIEWS. A CLOCKWISE JOURNEY WHICH CLIMBS GENTLY TO THE HEIGHTS BEFORE TRAVERSING THE KNOBBLY CREST AND DARK PERVASIVE FORESTRY ABOVE WINDERMERE LAKE.

INTRODUCTION

Moss Eccles Tarn

STEP BY STEP

▲ Descend the road through the village to find a surfaced lane rising to the right. Bear left, as lane rises to a red-roofed house, to cross a tiny footbridge. Continue to a junction with the track which rises from Low Sawrey. Keep right, ascending the stony track to pass rock outcrops to the left at which point lovely Moss Eccles Tarn lies to the left. Rise on the main track to observe Wise Een Tarn ahead. A stunning view extends to Langdale Pikes.

▲ Pass beneath the little upper tarn and make ascent to a junction with a stone wall. Go through the gate into the forestry to pass the boggy hollow of High Moss. At a junction bear right on the main track and continue to a bend to go right again (signed 'Ferry, Far Sawrey'). A footpath, with marker posts, heads into the forest. Follow it, passing an old lost stone wall until it snakes around to ascend to the summit of the rocky knoll of Claife Heights.

Low Pate Crag, Lake Windermere below

36

Recent thinning of the forestry gives an indication of what this once-famous viewpoint has to offer – a little more pruning to the north would reveal its full glory.

The path descends through the forestry to gain a track. Bear right (boggy pond to right) to follow it for 100m before the path (signed) breaks away to the left. Continue until a cleared hill rises to the west. Ascend this to find the trig point of High Blind How.

▲ Descend to the path beyond and twist around to the distinctive rock of High Pate Crag. Go left, descending to a level path from which a gap in a stone wall leads out along the promontory of Low Pate Crag; a heartwarming view over Windermere Lake. Return to the path and head south, keeping the stone wall to the left. Continue along the track until, after passing a small tarnlet beyond the final clearing of firs, the track forks. Go right and make descent. Finally go left down the leafy lane.

High Pate Crag

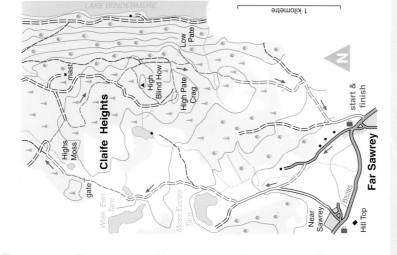

Far Sawrey

WALK 12 FACT FILE

START & FINISH: FAR SAWREY VILLAGE HALL (379955)

MAPS: OS L96 OR OL7

ACCESS: FROM AMBLESIDE FOLLOW THE A593 CONISTON ROAD TO TURN LEFT AT CLAPPERSGATE AND FOLLOW THE B5286.

TURN LEFT AT HAWKSHEAD TO FIND FAR SAWREY IN A FURTHER 4KM

WATERING HOLES: SAWREY HOTEL WITHIN THE VILLAGE

LENGTH: 8KM

TIME: 3 HOURS

DIFFICULTY: DIFFICULT; DESPITE MARKER POSTS THE FORESTRY SECTION IS DEMANDING IN TERMS OF BOTH ROUTE FINDING AND PHYSICAL EFFORT

AROUND TROUTBECK'S TONGUE

Limefitt Park, Long Green Head, The Tongue, High Street Roman Road, Trout Beck, Ancient Settlements, Clapper Bridge, Troutbeck Park, Ing Bridge

INTRODUCTION

5KM NORTH OF AMBLESIDE. RISING AND FALLING FROM TROUTBECK'S CULTIVATED LOWER REGIONS THIS ROUTE FOLLOWS THE LINE OF THE ROMAN ROAD BEFORE CONTINUING TO ROUND THE WILDS OF THE TONGUE. A RIVER CROSSING, A VISIT TO ANCIENT SETTLEMENTS, AND A STONE-SLAB CLAPPER BRIDGE COLOUR THE UPPER SECTION OF THE ROUND.

INTRODUCTION

The track up Troutbeck

STEP BY STEP

▲ Pass the church, old school and three stone wells until the way leads right through Limefitt Park caravan site. Cross the bridge, over the crystal-clear waters of Trout Beck (still known for its seasonal migration of sea trout and salmon), to ascend and pass the buildings.

▲ Discover a lane and go left along it continuing to traverse the fellside to the east side of the valley. Follow this track, passing above Long Green Head farm and continue, to cross a small ford below a barn before entering the narrowing valley formed by the protuberance of the Tongue to the left. Keep on the track beneath the slate-quarry spoil heaps to bear left over footbridges, to join the track rising from Troutbeck Park farm by the old barn buildings. This track constitutes the southern end of the famous high-level 'High Street Roman Road'.

▲ Rise with the track and pass through a gate. Go left through another gate to quit the track and follow the open rough-fell ground down to make a crossing of the Trout Beck. A boulder below a bend in the river makes a useful crossing point though other possibilities exist. Note in wet weather a safe crossing may be impossible. On the far side of the river, best

The Tongue above Troutbeck Park Farm

viewed when the bracken has died back, a number of mounds, arranged boulders and intercrossing stone walls suggest ancient settlement sites originating from various periods of prehistory.

Rise to take the gap in the stone wall and take the boggy grass track which falls to cross the beck by an ancient clapper bridge whose five spans consist of great stone slabs. The track, dreadfully muddy in places, falls through the mixed alder woods to enter Troutbeck Park farm. Pass left in front of the farm and follow the lane over Hagg Bridge and then Ing Bridge, over Trout Beck, from whence it becomes surfaced. As it rises up the hill to Town End keep left to follow the delightful little bridleway back to the main road. Down the hill to home.

Troutbeck clapper bridge

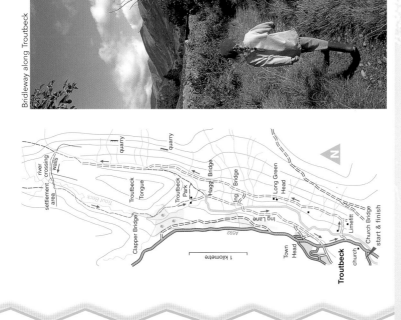

Bridleway along Troutbeck

WALK 13 FACT FILE

OVERALL GRADE

START & FINISH: TROUTBECK VALLEY, PARKING ABOVE THE RIVER BELOW CHURCH BRIDGE (412027)

MAPS: OS L90 OR OL7

ACCESS: FROM THE MINI-ROUNDABOUT ON THE A591 JUST BELOW (1KM NORTH OF) WINDERMERE ASCEND THE A592 INTO THE TROUTBECK VALLEY

WATERING HOLES: THE MORTAL MAN AND THE QUEEN'S HEAD WITHIN TROUTBECK

LENGTH: 13KM

TIME: 5 HOURS

DIFFICULTY: DIFFICULT; MAINLY ON GOOD TRACKS WITH EASY ASCENT, THOUGH A RIVER CROSSING, BOGGY GOING AND THE TOTAL LENGTH CONTRIBUTE TO THE

Map labels: quarry, quarry, river crossing, settlement area, walls, Troutbeck Tongue, Troutbeck Park, Hagg Bridge, Ing Bridge, Long Green Head, Clapper Bridge, Trout Beck, Ing Lane, A592, Town Head, Limefitt, Church Bridge, church, start & finish, **Troutbeck**, N, 1 kilometre

ORREST HEAD ABOVE WINDERMERE

Elleray Wood, leafy lanes, overgrown gardens, Elleray Bank, Orrest Head

Elleray Woods

INTRODUCTION

WINDERMERE. MIXED WOODS AND THE OVERGROWN OPULENT INTRIGUE OF A GRAND GARDEN GONE WILD CONTRAST DRAMATICALLY WITH WONDERFUL OPEN VISTAS OVER LAKE WINDERMERE. A SIMPLE ASCENT AND DESCENT OF ORREST HEAD ABOVE WINDERMERE TOWN.

STEP BY STEP

▶ The walk as described is very sim ple. Deliberately so. For, although you can easily extend the route by a number of options, it would seem superfluous to do so. Take the surfaced road, signed Orrest Head. After 50m the route bears off left to follow a track through the woods.

▶ Continue to a junction and turn right. A stony lane, between walls luxuriant in green moss, leads off left to climb the hill towards Elleray Bank. At the start, a faint path will be noted coming from the right, and above this the overgrown remains of a formal kitchen garden (presumably for the great house Elleray, now St Ann's School, down below). Just before the wood/field boundary on Elleray Bank, deep in over-grown rhododendrons, it is most interesting to zig right on the track before zagging back left at a higher level.

▶ With open view to the left climb the bank, through the stand of tall Scots pine, by the boundary until the way levels and quits the wood by a lane. Follow the lane until an iron kissing gate leads between two inscribed slate blocks and out onto the open rise of Orrest Head. Short

Orrest Head, view south west down Lake Windermere

40

Orrest Head, view north (top) and north-west

ascent leads to the summit. One stone dated 1902 thanks the Heywood family for gifting it to the people of Windermere. I'll second that. The view is astonishing, breathtaking. Over the nearly 18km length of Lake Windermere, from head to foot, the panorama includes the distant Pennines, Morecambe Bay and a magnificent array of fells, not least Coniston Old Man, Scafell, Bowfell, Langdale Pikes, Ullscarf, Red Screes and Thornthwaite Beacon.

In descent follow the lane back to the wood but then keep left at its edge, falling directly to join a surfaced lane which proves to be the original taken in ascent. Old guidebooks refer to the view from Orrest Head as 'the finest extensive view point in Great Britain'. Of course in this enlightened age of jet travel that may be considered a little inaccurate. It's much better than that.

WALK 14 FACT FILE

LENGTH: 2KM

TIME: 1¼ HOURS

DIFFICULTY: EASY, WITH MODERATE ASCENT AND DESCENT

START & FINISH: ABOVE THE A591 AT WINDERMERE (413988), LIMITED PARKING ON THE OPPOSITE SIDE OF THE ROAD

MAPS: OS L96 OR OL7

ACCESS: DIRECTLY ABOVE THE A591 JUST BELOW WINDERMERE HOTEL AND BUS PULL-OFF POINT, VIRTUALLY OPPOSITE THE RAILWAY STATION, A SURFACED ROAD CLIMBS TO ELLERAY

WATERING HOLES: WINDERMERE HOTEL, BOOTH'S SUPERMARKET TEA SHOP BY RAILWAY STATION

SCOUT SCAR FROM HELSINGTON CHURCH

Helsington Barrows, Scout Scar, The Bandstand, Barrowfield, Honeybee Wood, Wells Garth

Windy Howe

INTRODUCTION

5KM SOUTH-WEST OF KENDAL. FOUND AT THE SOUTH-EAST EDGE OF THE LAKES AND NOTED FOR ITS EXPANSIVE VIEWS, GEOLOGICAL AND BOTANICAL INTEREST, SCOUT SCAR IS A WONDERFULLY ELEVATED LIMESTONE EDGE. FROM HELSINGTON CHURCH THIS ROUTE GAINS AND TRAVERSES THE SCAR BEFORE DROPPING TO MAKE RETURN THROUGH HONEYBEE WOOD.

STEP BY STEP

▲ With the Kent Estuary at its foot, the Lyth Valley beneath, and a fine panorama of Lakeland fells framing its western and northern horizons, Scout Scar, running due north to south, provides an outing of considerable natural ambience. The windbent yews and whitebeam which cling to the white limestone cliff edge offer stark contrast to the sparsely grassed stony summit shoulder. The latter is complete with exotic orchids and butterflies in the summer months.

▲ Walk the lane back to the Brigsteer road and on reaching it bear right, climbing for a short way to a kissing gate on the left. Beyond the gate take the low grassy ancient trackway which climbs Helsington Barrows. Pass through the stone wall and continue to a further wall where the route is forced up to the right along the wall. Beyond the end of the wall cross a ditch, now overgrown with ash and thorn (an ancient trackway) and climb up to the pass which runs left along the rim of the scar.

▲ Continue along the edge of the scar to pass the dip and cairn above Barrowfield Farm. Keep along or near the edge, a choice of routes, for another 1200m to gain the unmistakable shelter known locally as 'The Bandstand'.

By Helsington Church

▲ Drop right, down the road for a few metres, until a narrow lane leads off south. At the junction ascend left to pass by a house above the hamlet of Wells Garth. A gate leads to a muddy track and open field above. A little way up the track it is possible to bear left making diagonal ascent up the field back to Helsington Church (an ancient trackway now invisible on the ground).

Scout Scar Millennium Dome!

On Scout Scar

To Scout Scar

▲ Make return to the cairn above Barrowfield Farm and find a recessed track dipping to make a zigzag descent into the trees. At the farm go left and take the track and signed path leading through the mixed limestone woodlands of Honeybee Wood to the Brigsteer road.

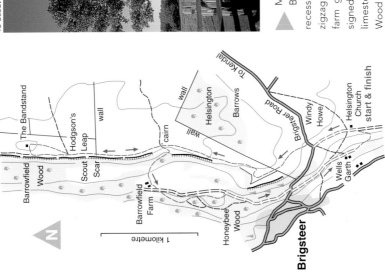

(Map showing: The Bandstand, Barrowfield Wood, Hodgson's Leap, Scout Scar, wall, cairn, Barrowfield Farm, Honeybee Wood, Brigsteer, Wells Garth, Helsington, Barrows, Windy Howe, Brigsteer Road, Helsington Church start & finish, To Kendal, N, 1 kilometre)

WALK 15 FACT FILE

START & FINISH: PARKING OPPOSITE HELSINGTON CHURCH (489889)

MAPS: OS L90 OR OL7/PATHFINDER 627

ACCESS: TAKE THE BRIGSTEER ROAD RISING FROM KENDAL. TURN LEFT TO THE CHURCH AS DESCENT IS MADE TO BRIGSTEER

WATERING HOLES: NONE EN ROUTE

LENGTH: 8KM

TIME: 2½ HOURS

DIFFICULTY: MODERATE, EASY ASCENT, MODERATE DESCENT. UNFENCED CLIFFS

AROUND THE VALE OF WINSTER

Winster House, Birket Houses Wood, Rulbuts Hill, Stonehills Tarn, Thorneyfields, Bow Mabble Breast

INTRODUCTION

7.5KM SOUTH OF AMBLESIDE. AT THE GEOLOGICAL MEETING OF DARK SILURIAN SLATE AND WHITE CARBONIFEROUS LIMESTONE. THE LOVELY WOODS AND ROLLING RIDGES AROUND THE VALE OF WINSTER PROVIDE DELIGHTFUL WALKING. THE ROUTE FIRST RISES TO THE WEST ABOVE WINDERMERE LAKE BEFORE DIPPING OVER THE VALLEY TO RISE AGAIN TO THE EAST.

Enclosed mixed wood, Winster

STEP BY STEP

▲ Autumn fruits found include damsons, crab apples, hazel nuts, sloe berries, blackberries, elderberries (edible), conkers and acorns (inedible). Towards Winster, a stile on the left enters a little field. Follow the path into the woods and continue through the trees to leave by a stile over a wire fence. Down through the field until the path gains the bridge over the little River Winster.

▲ Continue by the wall and on, to enter the next field. To the right are two walled enclosures of mixed woods and to the left, behind the trees, Birket Houses. Ascend the field to gain a track, and go left along the lane which leads behind Birket Houses. Emerge onto a surfaced track and immediately turn right to pass Winster House.

▲ Keep right and make ascent of the paved lane through Birket House Wood to emerge onto a rougher track which runs along the open spine. Go right until joined by another track falling from the left. Rulbuts Hill stands above. Views from the top extend over Windermere Lake to the high Lakeland fells. The track falls to a further junction above the farm of High House. From here follow the higher track which heads north. After passing into the open, bear right to intercept the A5074.

From Rulbuts Hill over Winster

Cross the road to continue along the lane. Cross the surfaced minor road of Lindeth Lane before following a track which rises to pass Stonehills Tarn. A long stony descent leads to a surfaced road. Go right, then left at the junction, to follow the surfaced road towards Gilpin Mill. At the apex of the zigzag bend, a lane leads off right to Thorneyfields.

Keep along this and descend to a barn on the right (farmhouse below). Go right and follow the grassy trackway over the rise, with the tree-lined limestone-scar Bow Mabble Breast to the right. Keep over the brow of the hill until in descent, boggy in places, the A5074 is again intercepted. Cross to Crag Lane and follow to a junction with the original surfaced minor road opposite Bryan House Farm. Right to finish.

Thorneyfields Farm

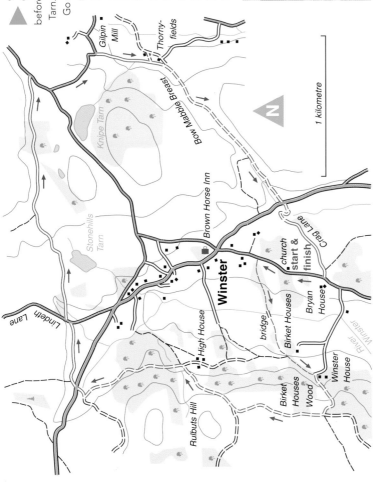

WALK 16 FACT FILE

START & FINISH: PARKING OPPOSITE WINSTER CHURCH (417931)

MAPS: OS L97 OR OL7

ACCESS: FOLLOW THE A5074 FROM WINDERMERE TO TURN RIGHT OPPOSITE THE BROWN HORSE INN IN WINSTER

WATERING HOLES: NONE EN ROUTE, BROWN HORSE INN NEARBY

LENGTH: 9KM

TIME: 3½ HOURS

DIFFICULTY: MODERATE, MILDLY STRENUOUS ASCENT THOUGH MOSTLY ON REASONABLE TRACKS

BY SELSIDE AND BETHECAR MOOR ABOVE CONISTON WATER

Grass Paddocks Wood, Parkamoor Track, Selside, Bethecar Moor, High Nibthwaite

INTRODUCTION. RISING FROM WOODED SLOPE TO COMMANDING POSITION ABOVE CONISTON WATER THIS ROUTE TRAVERSES THE BRACKENED AND HEATHER SECLUSION OF FELL AND MOOR. A 9KM SOUTH OF CONISTON. CLOCKWISE ROUND CLIMBING TO THE PARKAMOOR TRACK BEFORE TRAVERSING OPEN ROUGH FELL AND DESCENDING TO NIBTHWAITE TO MAKE RETURN ALONG THE LAKESIDE ROAD.

INTRODUCTION

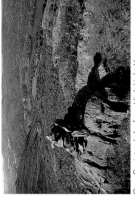

Over Coniston Lake from High Light Haw

STEP BY STEP

▲ From the head of the car park a track leads up through the woods, first curving to the left, then rising more steeply to the right. The path levels by a section of conifers, to cross a small stream before turning left at the fork and rising again. A stile leads suddenly out of the woods and onto the stony track of the High Nibthwaite to Parkamoor Farm road.

▲ Climb the track and follow it until, after passing the walled enclosure of Raises above to the right, it levels to traverse the hillside with an expansive view over Peel Island and Coniston Water. After the road drops and rises slightly a steep unworn-green grassy track joins it from the right. Take this track, rising until it levels to cross the open extensively brackened shelf. Cross two small streams, the latter falling from Arnsbarrow Tarn to become the head of Selside Beck, to climb past a rock slab with a surveyor's benchmark arrow chiselled in place. Climb to a rocky high point, before descent leads past a little crescent-shaped quarry.

▲ Beyond this the rocky shoulder of High Light Haw meets the path from the right. A worthwhile excursion may be made to this cairned viewpoint. Return by the same route is recommended. Continue along the track to cross the stream and find a natural rocky corridor which leads down

46

Looking to Peel Island, Coniston Water from Parkamoor Track

to a stone wall. Turn right and follow along the wall to make steep descent. Cross a track, after which the path falls to the high bank of Caws Beck.

Keep with the wall until a few boulders lead across the beck. The path continues to fall beneath the craggy face of Brock Barrow, rounding the flank of the hill and descending to the Parkamoor Farm road as it leaves Nibthwaite. Go through the gate into the hamlet and turn right to take a shortcut back to the road. Follow this past the beech woods of Water Park and the fields which open to a lovely aspect over the lake.

Caws Beck

High Nibthwaite

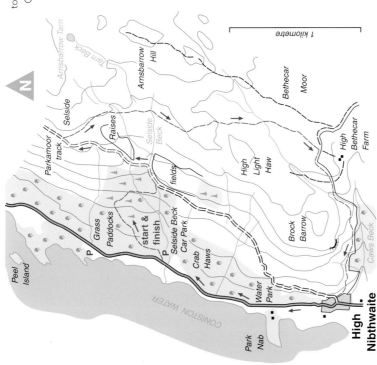

WALK 17 FACT FILE

LENGTH: 6KM

TIME: 3¾ HOURS

DIFFICULTY: MODERATE, FAIRLY STRENUOUS AND A LITTLE BOGGY IN PLACES

START & FINISH: SELSIDE BECK NATIONAL TRUST CAR PARK (296909)

MAPS: OS L97 OR OL6

ACCESS: FROM CONISTON TAKE THE B5285 HAWKSHEAD ROAD TURNING OFF RIGHT TO FOLLOW THE MINOR ROAD ALONG THE BACK OF CONISTON WATER

WATERING HOLES: NONE EN ROUTE. FARMERS ARMS AT LOWICK GREEN NEARBY

TORVER BACK COMMON AND CONISTON SHORE

Kelly Hall Tarn, Long Moss Tarn, Torver Common Wood, West Shore Coniston Water

By Long Moss Tarn

INTRODUCTION

5KM SOUTH OF CONISTON. THE OPEN-ACCESS
LAND OF TORVER BACK COMMON PROVIDES A
DELIGHTFUL ENVIRONMENT OF TARN, BRACKENED
HILL AND JUNIPER WITH VIEWS OVER CONISTON
WATER TO HIGH FELLS NEAR AND FAR. THIS ROUND
CROSSES THE HIGH COMMON BEFORE FALLING
THROUGH OAK WOODS TO TRAVERSE THE WEST
SHORE OF THE LAKE.

INTRODUCTION

STEP BY STEP

▲ Climb the track above the parking space to a kissing gate which leads onto the open hilly common. The grassy path bears left by Kelly Hall Tarn before rising to the right to round the flank of the hill and overlook Long Moss Tarn. A high path traverses above the southern shore of the tarn to swing left and cross the stream, continuing over boggy ground to rise to the left. To the right stands a series of rocky knolls. The highest knoll offers an excellent view to the Coniston fells and out over the head of Coniston Water to Fairfield and Red Screes.

▲ Regain the path and follow it in descent, entering the juniper and moving left to cross a little stream in a depression. Swing left out of this and contour the hillside below the stone wall, keeping left along a grassy track. This in turn, at a point where a footpath from Brackenbarrow Farm joins from the left, falls to a wooded depression through Torver Common Wood. A natural fault between the beds of outcropping rocks, it runs down to an open field by the side of Coniston Water.

Over Coniston Water to Torver Back Common

48

Gain the path just above the shoreline and head south through the woods. Note the presence of charcoal and iron bloom, a distinctly heavy purple-blue slag, and, camouflaged in the woods, the intriguing evidence of an industry many centuries past. Continue until the path pulls away from the shore, rising with a stone wall to the left. Take the high path which leads to the edge of the stone-walled enclosure of Delicars above. Follow the wall to exit onto the main road. Right to finish.

Over Coniston Water to Fairfield and Red Pike

WALK 18 FACT FILE

LENGTH: 6KM

TIME: 2½ HOURS

DIFFICULTY: MODERATE, EASY DESCENT AND ASCENT, MUDDY IN PLACES

START & FINISH: PARKING ABOVE THE A5084 OPPOSITE HADWIN'S LAND-ROVER GARAGE (287932)

MAPS: OS L97 OR OL6

ACCESS: LEAVE CONISTON ON THE A593, TURN RIGHT AT TORVER ALONG THE A5084 ULVERSTON ROAD

WATERING HOLES: NONE EN ROUTE. CHURCH HOUSE INN AT TORVER NEARBY

BY BROUGHTON'S APPLETREE WORTH AND THE RIVER LICKLE

Appletree Worth Deserted Farm, Pine Forest, River Lickle, Ancient Kilns, Stephenson Ground

INTRODUCTION

6KM SOUTH-WEST OF CONISTON. FALLING FROM
HIGH FELLS ABOVE THE DUDDON ESTUARY THE TWO
BECKS OF APPLETREE WORTH AND THE LICKLE
DEFINE A STEEPLY FALLING NOSE OF NOW
AFFORESTED GROUND. FOLLOWING FORESTRY
TRACKS, AN ANCIENT PATH AND TRACKWAY THIS
ROUTE MAKES AN INTRIGUING ROUND THROUGH
FOREST AND BY SECRETIVE DALE.

View to the Hawk (right) and the River Lickle (centre)

Footbridge over River Lickle

STEP BY STEP

▲ With the tumbled boulders and mossy banks of Appletree Worth Beck to the right, follow the forestry track into the trees. Strategically hidden atop the large steep bank to the left, lie the earth and stone works of the ancient settlement of the Hawk. Round the bend, with open field and hill to the right. At a point where the track rises from the beck, note on the far side the roofless ruins of the abandoned farm of Appletree Worth. Care should be taken in exploration as its stability is questionable.

▲ Rising with the track a larger forestry track is immediately intercepted. Cross this to find a rough path which rises through the forest between the junction of beech and larch trees. An old stone wall lies to the right and the path strikes a line below and parallel to this. Continue over the bridge of the hill, passing wind-blown trees, until descent leads to forestry track once again.

▲ Bear right and follow the track ascending gently with the deep tree-filled gorge of the River Lickle tumbling to the left. As the forestry begins to clear and (visible at the time of writing) high to the right the

Above River Lickle

Kiln above Stephenson Ground

craggy shape of Jordan Crag, surrounded by old Scots pine, can be seen. At this point a track cuts off down to the left and leads to a slate-slab bridge over the River Lickle.

Cross this and after short ascent bear left along the track, running across the pleasantly open fellside, which forms the west bank of the river. In places, see where tracks worn deep into the outcropping rocks. The track bears away from the gorge, first rising before falling to the stone buildings of Stephenson Ground. Before reaching the buildings, with stone wall to the left, an ancient kiln of circular construction stands to the right.

A gate opens to the surfaced road. Bear left and descend this, observing another stone kiln to the left just prior to crossing Water Yeat Bridge. Follow the pleasantly wooded lane easily back to Hawk Bridge.

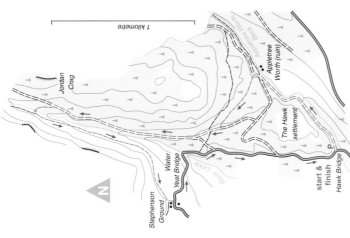

N

1 kilometre

Jordan Crag

Stephenson Ground

Water Yeat Bridge

River Lickle

Appletree Worth (ruin)

Appletree Worth Beck

The Hawk settlement

start & finish

P

Hawk Bridge

WALK 19 FACT FILE

LENGTH: 5.5KM

TIME: 1½ HOURS

DIFFICULTY: EASY GOING MAINLY ON TRACKS OR ROAD WITH ONE SHORT SECTION OF ROUGH PATH

START & FINISH: HAWK BRIDGE CAR PARK (239920)

MAPS: OS L96 OR OL6

ACCESS: FROM CONISTON FOLLOW THE A593 SOUTH THROUGH TORVER UNTIL IN 5KM A MINOR ROAD (BROUGHTON MOOR, BEWARE OF QUARRY TRAFFIC) RISES STEEPLY TO THE RIGHT. FOLLOW THIS TO CROSSROADS ABOVE BROUGHTON MILLS AND BEAR RIGHT

WATERING HOLES: THE BLACKSMITH'S ARMS INN AT BROUGHTON MILLS

SEATHWAITE TARN FROM THE DUDDON'S BIRKS BRIDGE

Pike How, Seathwaite Tarn, Long House, Tongue House, Troutal Tongue, Birks Bridge

INTRODUCTION

16KM SOUTH-WEST OF AMBLESIDE. HIGH IN THE FELLS ABOVE THE TUMBLING RIVER DUDDON NESTLE THE DAMMED WATERS OF SEATHWAITE TARN. BEGINNING BY THE RIVERSIDE THIS ROUND RISES BY WOOD AND OPEN FELL TO GAIN THE TARN, THEN FALLS, ONLY TO RISE ONCE AGAIN OVER TROUTAL TONGUE, AND ON TO BIRKS BRIDGE.

INTRODUCTION

Descent track to Seathwaite Tarn

STEP BY STEP

▲ Leave the car park and turn left along the road. (Note Birks Bridge lies downstream of the car park.) In 200m follow a forestry track which bears off to the right. Round a bend to find a little track rising to the right (waymarked). Follow it and on over Pike How. Descend through the trees to gain the head of a little valley (the Close).

▲ Go left, over the stream and rise by the ruined wall. Cross the stile and ascend steeply until, with crags above, a path traverses out to the right. Keep along this until a gap appears in the stone wall. Go through the gap and bear right before swinging left and ascending by a crag. Follow the way-marked path above Tarn Beck, boggy in places, to gain the end of the dam.

▲ With the impressively wild aspect of Seathwaite Tarn above, cross the metal walkways and out onto the curving concrete wall of the dam. At its end follow the track to traverse the hillside before making descent. Near the bottom of the hill a gate leads off right to a stone-walled lane which falls directly to the buildings of Long House. Go through these

Seathwaite Tarn high amongst the fells

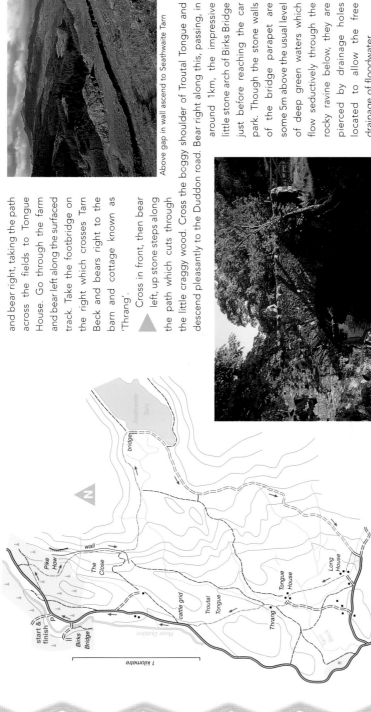

Above gap in wall ascend to Seathwaite Tarn

Birks Bridge

and bear right, taking the path across the fields to Tongue House. Go through the farm and bear left along the surfaced track. Take the footbridge on the right which crosses Tarn Beck and bears right to the barn and cottage known as 'Thrang'.

▲ Cross in front, then bear left, up stone steps along the path which cuts through the little craggy wood. Cross the boggy shoulder of Troutal Tongue and descend pleasantly to the Duddon road. Bear right along this, passing, in around 1km, the impressive little stone arch of Birks Bridge just before reaching the car park. Though the stone walls of the bridge parapet are some 5m above the usual level of deep green waters which flow seductively through the rocky ravine below, they are pierced by drainage holes located to allow the free drainage of floodwater.

WALK 20 FACT FILE

LENGTH: 9KM

TIME: 3 HOURS

DIFFICULTY: DIFFICULT, MODERATELY STRENUOUS ASCENTS AND BOGGY IN PLACES

START & FINISH: BIRKS BRIDGE CAR PARK (235995)

MAPS: OS L96 OR OL6

ACCESS: FROM AMBLESIDE FOLLOW THE A593 CONISTON ROAD TO TURN RIGHT (IN 5KM) TO LITTLE LANGDALE. CONTINUE OVER MOUNTAINOUS WRYNOSE PASS TO TURN LEFT AT COCKLEY BECK, DESCENDING THE DUDDON VALLEY

WATERING HOLES: NONE EN ROUTE. THE NEWFIELD INN AT SEATHWAITE NEARBY

ULPHA PARK ABOVE THE DUDDON

Ulpha Bridge, Millbrow, Bleabeck Bridge, Frith Hall, Logan Beck Bridge, Beckfoot, Forge Wood

INTRODUCTION

25KM SOUTH-WEST OF AMBLESIDE. IN ULPHA PARK, OCCUPYING FINE POSITION ABOVE THE LOWER DUDDON, STANDS THE NOTORIOUS RUIN OF FRITH HALL. MAKING A CIRCUIT FROM ULPHA BRIDGE RISING BY MILLBROW TO FOLLOW AN ANCIENT PACK-HORSE ROUTE, THIS WALK PASSES FRITH HALL BEFORE FALLING TO BECKFOOT AND RETURNING BY THE DELIGHTFUL WOODS OF THE DUDDON.

Ulpha Bridge

STEP BY STEP

▲ The gaunt ruins of Frith Hall stand skeletal-like and mysterious above the intoxicating charms of the lower Duddon Valley. Dry facts say that it was built in 1608 and later became an inn serving the packhorse route to Millom. Local legend tells of intrigue, murder and hauntings. Over Ulpha Bridge turn left and follow the road over the bridge, past the Mill cottages, and up the hill to turn left along the old packhorse route traversing Millbrow.

▲ The lane, offering an expansive view over the Duddon, continues over Bleabeck Bridge to pass Frith Hall. Framed by the shapely fells of Great Stickle, Caw and Dow Crag beyond, the hall with its ruined tower and great gable ends is both imposing and impressively situated. The track continues, passing the end of the nearby

Over Frith Hall

ULPHA
Ulpha Bridge
school
start & finish

N

Millbrow
mill
Frith Hall
Forge Wood
Booth Holme
Middle Park
Ulpha Park
New Plantation
Penn
Low Park
Beck-foot
Beckstones
Logan Beck Bridge
cattle grid
River Duddon

1 kilometre

Frith Hall

two stone barns (one also ruinous) before entering the dark conifer wood. Over the top of the hill descent leads to Logan Beck Bridge.

▲ Bear left along the surfaced road. Go left again at the junction, descending until a track leads off through the higher buildings of Beckfoot. On over the stone-arched bridge, re-crossing Logan Beck, to bear left through the lower buildings.

▲ With the River Duddon to the right the track continues by the deciduous trees of Low Park, Middle Park and Forge Wood before finally rising to emerge onto the original surfaced road opposite the Mill cottages. In springtime, spread beneath these once-coppiced woods, note the carpet of precious pale yellow – one of the last and perhaps the most important stronghold of the indigenous Lakeland daffodil. Smaller, sweeter, than the usual daffodil its survival depends on us – please don't pick them.

Bleabeck Bridge

WALK 21 FACT FILE

LENGTH: 10KM
TIME: 2½ HOURS
DIFFICULTY: MODERATE, EASY ASCENT AND DESCENT, GOOD TRACKS THROUGHOUT
START & FINISH: ULPHA BRIDGE, PARKING OPPOSITE THE SCHOOL (197930)
MAPS: OS L96 OR OL6
ACCESS: FROM AMBLESIDE FOLLOW THE A593 CONISTON ROAD TO TURN RIGHT (IN 5KM) TO LITTLE LANGDALE. CONTINUE OVER MOUNTAINOUS WRYNOSE PASS TO TURN LEFT AT COCKLEY BECK, DESCENDING THE DUDDON VALLEY
WATERING HOLES: NONE EN ROUTE. THE NEWFIELD INN AT SEATHWAITE NEARBY

THE CIRCUIT OF DEVOKE WATER

Birker Fell, Tewit Moss, Devoke Water, Burial Cairns, Watness Coy, Washfold Point, Seat How

INTRODUCTION

25KM WEST OF CONISTON. BETWEEN THE DUDDON AND ESKDALE, HIDDEN ON THE WILD EXPANSE OF BIRKER FELL WHERE THE FELLS FINALLY FALL TO THE WEST COAST, LIE THE MOODY WATERS OF DEVOKE. THIS WALK ENCIRCLES THE TARN WITH VIEWS TO THE GREAT SCAFELLS AND TO THE DISTANT ISLE OF MAN.

STEP BY STEP

The tarn lies unseen from the road until it levels to cross the bleak expanse of Tewit Moss. The road was made-up in Victorian times to serve the solitary boathouse standing opposite Washfold Point. However, it has long been an important route, one which continues after the tarn to fall through the great Neolithic settlement of Barnscar before traversing the plains to gain Hall Waberthwaite – the strategic ford crossing point of the estuarine River Esk.

Shortly after the tarn comes into view, the track bears left to the boathouse. However, our route goes right to make an anti-clockwise round of the tarn. Stretched between heather and rough fell, open only to the east and west, Devoke Water presents a wild, treeless, aspect. Its occasional tranquillity is often violently shattered by the invading westerlies plying across the Irish Sea. A faint path leads along above its north shore, avoiding the boggy bits by ascending the flanks of Rough Crag and Water Crag as necessary. Cross the outlet stream of Rough Crag and Water Crag as necessary. Cross the outlet stream of Linbeck Gill, interestingly flanked by stone. Rise to the right, to a circular mound of stones topped by a little circular shelter. The shelter is of

To Devoke Water

Devoke Water looking west

comparatively recent origin; the pile of stones is probably a burial mound from around 5,000BC.

There is a number of such stone curiosities scattered around the tarn. Gain the better path by the south shore to pass the lone island of Watness Coy. Its windswept stand of scrubby trees are the only specimens to be found in the area. Continue, to skirt Washfold Point with a breathtaking view to the

distant heights of Scafell and the high fells arrayed around upper Eskdale.

A boggy section follows before the path rises to meet the track above the boathouse beneath the heights of Seat How. The boathouse itself is a splendid building, although sadly its outbuildings are now roofless. The silvered granite and blue volcanics used in its construction emphasise the geological meeting of the two rocks on this site.

Burial mound/shelter west end of Devoke Water

Over Devoke Water boathouse to Scafell beyond

MAP LABELS

To Ulpha

High Ground

start & finish

Birker Fell

Tewit Moss

Rough Crag

Seat How

boat house

cairns

Water Crag

Washfold Point

DEVOKE WATER

Watness Coy

cairns

N

1 kilometre

WALK 22 FACT FILE

LENGTH: 5KM

TIME: 1½ HOURS

DIFFICULTY: EASY, THOUGH VERY BOGGY

START & FINISH: PARKING AT THE JUNCTION BY THE SIDE OF THE BIRKER FELL ROAD (171977)

MAPS: OS L96 OR OL6

ACCESS: FOLLOW THE A593 FROM CONISTON, TURNING RIGHT ALONG THE A595 TO DUDDON BRIDGE, AND FOLLOW THE MINOR ROAD UP THE DUDDON TO TURN LEFT OVER THE BIRKER FELL ROAD ABOVE ULPHA

WATERING HOLES: NONE EN ROUTE. THE GREEN STATION IN NEARBY ESKDALE

STANLEY GILL FALLING TO THE RIVER ESK

Dalegarth Hall, Stanley Gill, Stanley Force (Dalegarth Force), Low Ground, Whincop

INTRODUCTION

25KM WEST OF AMBLESIDE. BIRKER BECK PLUNGES DRAMATICALLY FROM THE HEIGHTS THROUGH THE DEEP NARROW GRANITE GORGE OF STANLEY GILL AND DOWN TO THE RIVER ESK. VIEWING THE WATERFALL, STANLEY FORCE, AND MAKING A CIRCUIT AROUND STANLEY GILL AND ITS CATCHMENT, THIS WALK FIRST CLIMBS THE WEST BANK TO DESCEND BY THE EAST.

Stanley Force

STEP BY STEP

▲ Being dwarfed within the smooth, red-walled granite ravine of Stanley Gill, with its thundering waterfall, giant rhododendron, tall pine and lush fern, may give an impression of being within the Himalaya rather than in Eskdale. Follow the track from the car park. Turn left (Dalegarth Hall to the right), and continue through a meeting of the ways until a gate enters the woods on the left. A well-constructed path continues up the west bank of the beck to the 1st wooden footbridge.

▲ Cross this and continue through the deepening ravine, to recross the beck on a 2nd bridge. Follow the path on the west bank to a 3rd footbridge. To view the highest fall, cross this bridge to the east bank and follow the narrow ascending path to make an exposed traverse above steep unprotected (at the time of writing) ground which finally descends slightly to a platform and dramatic postion below sheer walls

To Low Ground above Stanley Gill

58

and opposite the waterfall and plunge pool.

▲ Retrace your steps, recross the 3rd bridge and follow steeply up the west bank of the gill between the trees. The path traverses the edge, unfenced drop, offering wonderful view over Eskdale to Scafell. A stile leads to open ground. Lane to Low Ground. Pass between the buildings and bear left at the junction, to follow the lane to Whincop Farm.

▲ Keep left of the farmhouse and continue on to follow the grassy track, until a stile leads over the wall. Fall by the stream until a gap can be seen in the corner of the meeting walls. Go through the gap to find an ancient trackway which leads down by the side of the wall. (Rather boggy and overgrown.) This leads to oak woods and a ladder stile over the wall. Continue through the woods, with a stone ruin to the right, to follow along a wall. Cross a stile to open ground. Short descent leads to a track. A gate on the left gains a wooden footbridge which crosses the beck. Continue across a field to the meeting of ways on the original track.

First bridge over Stanley Gill

To Whincop Farm

WALK 23 FACT FILE

START & FINISH: CAR PARK NEAR DALEGARTH HALL (171003)

MAPS: OS L96/89 OR OL6

ACCESS: FROM AMBLESIDE CROSS OVER WRYNOSE PASS AND HARDKNOTT PASS (SUMMER CONDITIONS ONLY) TO ESKDALE TO TURN LEFT PAST DALEGARTH STATION

WATERING HOLES: NONE EN ROUTE. DALEGARTH STATION AND THE BURNMOOR INN AT BOOT NEARBY

LENGTH: 4.5KM

TIME: 2½ HOURS

DIFFICULTY: MODERATE; SHORT STEEP ASCENT, BOGGY IN PLACES, UNFENCED DROPS REQUIRE CARE

MITERDALE AND THE STONE CIRCLES OF BURNMOOR

Low Place Farm, Miterdale Head, Burnmoor Tarn and Lodge, Brat's Moss Stone Circles

INTRODUCTION

30KM WEST OF AMBLESIDE. FALLING FROM SCAFELL, SECLUDED MITERDALE IS SET APART FROM WASDALE BY HIGH FELLS AND FROM ESKDALE BY THE SHOULDER OF BURN MOOR. RISING TO THE CANYON-LIKE HEAD OF MITERDALE THIS WALK CROSSES ABOVE BURNMOOR TARN BEFORE TRAVERSING THE MOOR, PASSING BY THREE STONE CIRCLES, TO FINALLY RETURN TO THE DALE.

Burnmoor Lodge above Burnmoor Tarn

STEP BY STEP

▶ Cross the bridge and continue up the track to Low Place Farm. Bear right noting in the stone wall opposite the beck the dialect sign 'HOD REET FUR ESHDEL' (Keep right for Eskdale). Cross the river, tricky stepping stones at the ford, or footbridge a little higher.

▶ Follow along the track which rises above the beck and continue, passing Bakerstead, and on over two stiles en route, until it becomes an open footpath. Follow the course of the stream, which first disappears then reappears, before entering the sunken canyon-like head of Miterdale. Surrounded by rock walls and fed by three water-falls, coupled with the stream disappearance and resurgence, it could be deduced that the visible volcanic rocks are actually underlain by limestone.

▶ Exit right, above a little crag, and make a leftward traverse across the hillside skirting above Burnmoor Barn to Burnmoor Lodge. Make direct ascent behind the building to find a grassy track which crosses the shoulder of Burn Moor. This track continues to traverse the Eskdale face of Boat How. As the track

Head of Miterdale

Larger stone circle on Burnmoor's Brat's Moss

Higher stone circle on Brat's Moss

swings left, two little stone circles appear ahead, and left of these, a larger circle. In terms of atmosphere and position the Brat's Moss stone circles make up for anything they lack in grandeur of scale.

Bear right, descending from the circles on a vague grassy path until a little climb intercepts a well-defined path. Left along this until, by the forestry, a path drops steeply down to the right back to Miterdale. Take the original track then bear right to the ruins of Miterdale Head Farm. Go left from here, crossing a footbridge to Bakerstead, then diagonally across the field to gain the lane which leads back to Low Place Farm.

WALK 24 FACT FILE

LENGTH: 11KM

TIME: 4 HOURS

DIFFICULTY: DIFFICULT; VARIED TERRAIN WITH SOME ASCENT, BOGGY IN PLACES

START & FINISH: END OF SURFACED ROAD IN MITERDALE (147012)

MAPS: OS L89 OR OL6

ACCESS: FROM AMBLESIDE CROSS OVER WRYNOSE PASS AND HARDKNOTT PASS (SUMMER CONDITIONS ONLY) TO ESKDALE CONTINUING TO ESKDALE GREEN, TURN RIGHT, PAST THE SCHOOL, TO ENTER MITERDALE

WATERING HOLES: NONE EN ROUTE. DALEGARTH STATION AND THE BOWERHOUSE INN NEARBY

PORT RAVENGLASS: WHERE THE ESK MEETS THE SEA

Port Ravenglass, Walls Castle, Muncaster Castle, River Esk, Esk Estuary

River Esk Estuary

INTRODUCTION

18KM S OF EGREMONT. LOCATED ON THE FINAL BEND OF THE RIVER ESK, AT THE LATTER'S CONFLUENCE WITH THE MITE AND IRT, THE ANCIENT PORT OF RAVENGLASS OCCUPIES PERFECT POSITION WITH HIGH SHOULDER ABOVE AND ESTUARY BELOW. ASCEND THE WOODED SHOULDER PASSING ROMAN WALLS CASTLE BEFORE FALLING TO FOLLOW THE RIVER ESK.

STEP BY STEP

▲ Note, Muncaster Castle Gardens, at their most splendid in May when the rhododendrons are in flower, are private and a 'Walker's Timed Ticket' must be purchased on entrance. This allows the walker to pass through the gardens and by the castle, for a small fee, with a stop-off at the café. Naturally protected from the Irish Sea by the sandspits and dunes of Drigg and Eskmeals, the estuarine Esk is a haven for seabirds. Served by La'al Ratty miniature railway from Eskdale (and by the main west coast line) this delightful route contrasts estuary mud and pebble with wood and primrose, including the additional attractions of Muncaster Castle and the Roman remains of Walls Castle.

▲ The main street through Ravenglass leads directly to the shore. Traverse the shore until in 300 metres a path leads left through the low underpass beneath the railway. Continue to a surfaced road then bear right to pass Walls Castle. Go left at the next two junctions and rise up through Decoy Woods. Follow the track through the field directly to the Castle Information Centre.

▲ Gain entrance and continue down the main drive to pass the castle and find the Riverside Drive track which descends, passing the

Muncaster Woods by the River Esk

Muncaster Castle

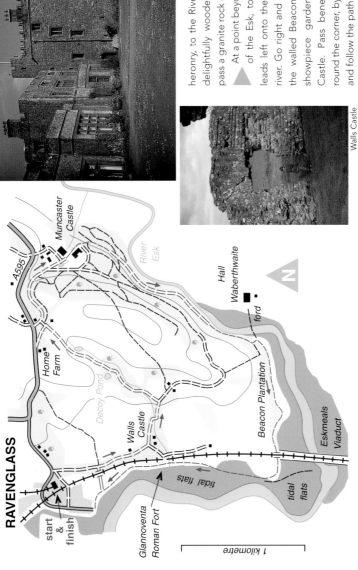

heronry, to the River Esk. Bear right along the delightfully wooded track above the river to pass a granite rock cutting with carved 'M 1882'.

▲ At a point beyond the ancient ford crossing of the Esk, to Hall Waberthwaite, a gate leads left onto the bank of the now estuarine river. Go right and follow the path, which skirts the walled Beacon Plantation woods, once a showpiece garden extension to Muncaster Castle. Pass beneath Eskmeals viaduct and round the corner, by the boundary fence, to gain and follow the path along the shoreline.

Walls Castle

WALK 25 FACT FILE

LENGTH: 9KM

TIME: 4 HOURS

DIFFICULTY: MODERATE; MAINLY LEVEL GOING ON REASONABLE PATHS, THE FIRST SECTION ALONG THE SHORE MAY BE IMPASSABLE AT HIGH TIDE.

START & FINISH: RAVENGLASS CENTRAL CAR PARK (085965)

MAPS: OS L89 OR OL6

ACCESS: FOUND JUST OFF THE MAIN WEST-COAST ROAD (A595)

WATERING HOLES: MUNCASTER CASTLE EN ROUTE, RATTY ARMS AND CAFE AT RAVENGLASS

RAVENGLASS

A595

Muncaster Castle

River Esk

Home Farm

Decoy Pond

Walls Castle

Hall Waberthwaite

ford

Beacon Plantation

Eskmeals Viaduct

tidal flats

tidal flats

Glannoventa Roman Fort

start & finish

N

1 kilometre

WASDALE HEAD

Wasdale Church, Burnthwaite, Mosedale Beck, Ritson's Force, Packhorse Bridge, Wasdale Head Inn

INTRODUCTION

42KM WEST OF AMBLESIDE. A PATCHWORK OF STONE-WALLED FIELDS, A TINY COMMUNITY NESTLING BENEATH AN UNRIVALLED STAND OF HIGH FELLS – THE MAGICAL MOUNTAIN SANCTUARY OF WASDALE HEAD. A SIMPLE ANTICLOCKWISE ROUND WHICH SOAKS UP THE ATMOSPHERE, ADMIRES THE VIEWS, AND VISITS A NUMBER OF POINTS OF INTEREST.

Wasdale Head

STEP BY STEP

▲ Wasdale Head has long been an important staging post, connecting three mountain passes to the coast. Moses' illicit whisky and the immensely valuable wad 'recovered' from the Seathwaite graphite mines came this way. With the railway age 'Auld' Will Ritson recognised the potential and extended his farm into what is now the Wasdale Head Inn. He most famously commented that Wasdale has 'the highest mountain, the deepest lake, the smallest church and the biggest liar in England'. A truism varying only with the winner of the biggest-liar competition at nearby Egremont Crab Fair. Wasdale was also the birthplace of rock climbing with W.P. Haskett-Smith's first ascent of Napes Needle in 1886.

▲ Take the stony lane which leads past the church, noting the thickness of the walls and the great piles of stones gathered to clear the land for cultivation, to pass through Burnthwaite. It is worth walking a few hundred metres to the right to obtain a wonderful uninterrupted view of the Napes Face of Great Gable towering high above the scree to the left.

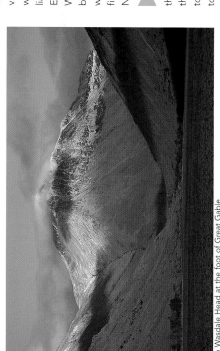
To Wasdale Head at the foot of Great Gable

64

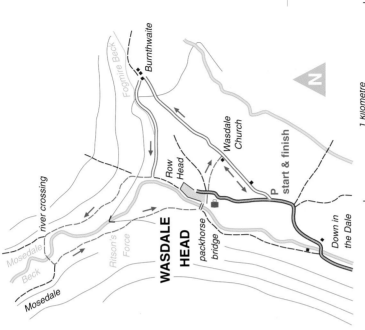

Wasdale Head packhorse bridge

▲ Make return and continue to gain and follow the lane following little Fogmire Beck. Numerous footbridges zigzag across the beck until a junction is made with the track descending from Mosedale. Bear right climbing the hill to enter Mosedale. As the stone wall bears off to the left and the valley opens swing left to make a crossing of the beck (dry conditions advised), to find a gate which provides access to the path on the west side of the valley.

▲ Follow the path and track until the hill is crested. A lesser path leads off the track, down to the left through the larch trees, to allow a viewing of the two-stage little waterfall of Ritson's Force. Return to the track and follow it to the ancient stone packhorse bridge. Cross and bear right until, by the Wasdale Head Inn, the way leads left to the end of the surfaced road. Bear left and then right to cross the fields to join the original lane by the church.

WALK 26 FACT FILE

LENGTH: 4KM

TIME: 2 HOURS

DIFFICULTY: EASY, THOUGH A RIVER CROSSING ADDS TO THE FUN

START & FINISH: COMMON GROUND AS THE TRACK FORKS TO BURNTHWAITE (187085)

MAPS: OS L89 OR OL6

ACCESS: GOSFORTH LIES JUST OFF THE MAIN WEST-COAST ROAD (A595) SOME 15KM SOUTH OF EGREMONT AND A MINOR ROAD LEADS FROM HERE TO WASDALE (14KM)

WATERING HOLES: WASDALE HEAD INN EN ROUTE

AROUND LOWESWATER

Hudson Place, Holme Wood, Watergate Farm, Maggie's Bridge, Thrushbank, Pinfold

Loweswater

16KM WEST OF KESWICK. HIGH ON THE NORTH-
WESTERN FRINGE OF THE LAKE DISTRICT,
LOWESWATER LIES IN A NARROW CORRIDOR
CUTTING THROUGH THE SURROUNDING FELLS. THIS
MAINLY LEVEL CIRCUIT OFFERS THE OPPORTUNITY
TO TREAD BOTH THE SOUTH AND NORTH SHORES
OF THE LAKE, CONTRASTING MIXED WOODLAND
WITH OPEN VIEWS.

STEP BY STEP

▲ Enchanting mixed woods, rich and varied bird life, and the open waters of Loweswater all contribute to make this walk a particularly fine outing. Head north-west down the road, Loweswater Hall stands largely hidden to the right, until a signed path leads left across the fields. Cross the fields via a stile and little wooden footbridge rising to the lane. Go left climbing to Hudson Place Farm. The date of 1741 above the door with the magnificent Scots pine in front suggest sympathy to the Jacobite cause.

▲ Continue descending the stony lane to enter the wonderful mixture of broad leaf and pine of Holme Wood. The main track is unmistakable and quite delightful, though many will opt to veer left and follow a lesser path by the shore of Loweswater. Pass the magically situated Holme Wood Bothy (let out by the National Trust) and continue along the track to exit the wood.

▲ The path steers left of Watergate Farm to regain the track and continues along it by Maggie's Bridge to the surfaced road. Climb the hill,

Grasmoor over Loweswater

66

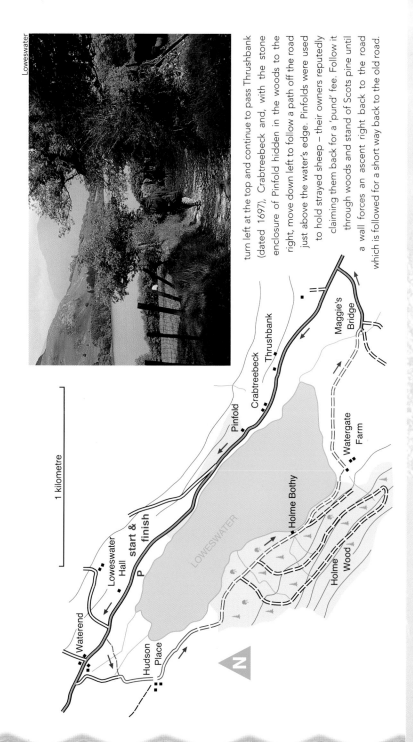

Loweswater

turn left at the top and continue to pass Thrushbank (dated 1697), Crabtreebeck and, with the stone enclosure of Pinfold hidden in the woods to the right, move down left to follow a path off the road just above the water's edge. Pinfolds were used to hold strayed sheep – their owners reputedly claiming them back for a 'pund' fee. Follow it through woods and stand of Scots pine until a wall forces an ascent right back to the road which is followed for a short way back to the old road.

W A L K 27 F A C T F I L E

LENGTH: 6KM

TIME: 3 HOURS

DIFFICULTY: EASY; INCLUDES A SHORT ROAD SECTION

START & FINISH: PARKING ON OLD ROAD (121223)

MAPS: OS L89 OR OL4

ACCESS: FROM KESWICK FOLLOW THE A66 TO BRANCH OFF THROUGH BRAITHWAITE TAKING THE B5292 THROUGH WHINLATTER PASS TO TURN LEFT ALONG THE B5289 AT LORTON, FINALLY BEARING RIGHT TO LOWESWATER

WATERING HOLES: NONE EN ROUTE, KIRKSTILE INN AT LOWESWATER NEARBY

THE ROUND OF BUTTERMERE

Shingle Point, Crag Wood, Hassness Tunnel, Buttermere Village, Sourmilk Gill, Peggy's Bridge

INTRODUCTION

13KM SOUTH-WEST OF KESWICK. PLACED BENEATH HIGH SUBLIME MOUNTAINS, PASSING THROUGH DELECTABLE MIXED WOODS AND OFFERING A CONSTANTLY CHANGING OPEN VISTA OVER THE EMERALD-GREEN WATERS OF BUTTERMERE LAKE, THIS IS ONE OF THE CLASSIC WALKS OF LAKELAND. A CIRCUIT WHICH PASSES THROUGH HASSNESS TUNNEL AND VISITS BUTTERMERE VILLAGE.

Hassness Tunnel, Buttermere

STEP BY STEP

▲ This round lacks nought for its simplicity or ease of execution and its beauty is simply spellbinding. Follow the road up the hill to pass the farm and continue along to reach the side of the lake. Take the path which traverses the shore to the flat slatey stones of Shingle Point. Beyond here the great Scots pine and mixed trees of Crag Wood lead to the short rock tunnel of Hassness (a torch is unnecessary).

▲ A little bay harbours a cluster of wooden clinker-built char boats before the path along Pike Rigg reaches the end of the lake. Keep along the path to pass through Wilkinsyke Farm and turn left to make short descent to Buttermere Village. (Alternatively a permissive path turns off left to follow by the shore along the bottom of the lake.)

▲ Pass the Bridge Inn and the Fish Inn, keeping left

Buttermere and Shingle Point below Birkness Combe

Boats on Buttermere

The head of Buttermere

BUTTERMERE

Pike Rigg

Dale-garth

Hassness Tunnel

start & finish

Gatesgarth Farm

Peggy's Bridge

Shingle Point

Horse Close

Burtness Wood

BUTTERMERE

Sourmilk Gill

N

1 kilometre

road section

along the track, with a fine view of the great tumbling waterfall of Sourmilk Gill ahead, to reach the shore of the lake once again. A bridge leads across the clear waters of Buttermere Dubs and the path followed left over a further bridge across the gill.

▲ The low path through the woods is a delight before it rises to leave the woods and traverses Horse Close to a junction with the Scarth Gap Pass. Go left, over Peggy's Bridge and follow the fields back to Gatesgarth Farm. A walk for all seasons.

WALK 28 FACT FILE

LENGTH: 7KM

TIME: 3 HOURS

DIFFICULTY: EASY; INCLUDES A SHORT ROAD SECTION

START & FINISH: PARKING OPPOSITE GATESGARTH FARM (195150)

MAPS: OS L89 OR OL4

ACCESS: TAKE THE A66 FROM KESWICK TURNING OFF AT PORTINSCALE TO FOLLOW THE NEWLANDS VALLEY AND OVER NEWLANDS PASS TO BUTTERMERE.

WATERING HOLES: THE BRIDGE AND THE FISH INNS AND A CAFE IN BUTTERMERE VILLAGE

THE HEAD OF BORROWDALE: SEATOLLER TO SEATHWAITE

Folly Bridge, Mountain View, Seathwaite, Sourmilk Gill, Borrowdale Yews, Seatoller Bridge

INTRODUCTION

12KM SOUTH OF KESWICK. THE HEAD OF THE LOVELY
BORROWDALE VALLEY, THAT FINAL STRETCH OF GREEN
FROM WHICH THE MOUNTAINS RISE, RUNS BETWEEN
THE HAMLETS OF SEATOLLER AND SEATHWAITE.
WITH FINE VIEWS TO THE MOUNTAINS AND NUMEROUS
POINTS OF INTEREST THIS ROUND CIRCUMNAVIGATES
THE VALLEY IN CLOCKWISE DIRECTION.

INTRODUCTION

River Derwent at Seathwaite

STEP BY STEP

A path leaves the back of the car park to cross a stile. Bear right and continue above the wall with the architecturally curious building of Glaramara below. Keep along through the large oaks until, at the end of the wall, the path descends to cross Folly Bridge. A slate headstone dates the bridge 1781 and is inscribed: 'I count this folly you have done, as you have neither wife nor son, daughter I have god give her grace, and heaven for her resting place'. An intriguing riddle or simple rhyme? Solutions by e-mail please.

Cross the field to pass the end of the Mountain View Cottages and cross the road beneath the hump-backed Strands Bridge, to take the lane opposite. Follow by the River Derwent and continue to bear left on the grassy lane/path at a point where the track swings right to Thorneythwaite. Easy going leads along the south side of the valley to the hamlet of Seathwaite.

Turn right down the cobbled lane between the buildings and then left to pass beneath a flat arch leading through the barn. Follow the lane to cross the bridge over the River Derwent beneath the waterfalls of Sourmilk Gill.

Glaramara, Seatoller

70

SEATOLLER

To Sourmilk Gill

Seathwaite Farm

Go right to cross the little gill by a further foot-bridge and continue down the northern side of the valley. Above to the left you can just discern the spoil heaps of the old plumbago mines. Worked for over 400 years, Seathwaite was once the only source of quality graphite in Europe – then an incredibly valuable mineral protected by armed guards.

In a matter of 300m the much-celebrated Borrowdale Yews stand just above the path to the left. Perhaps a thousand years old the largest tree has a girth of approximately 10m and is around 15m high; its bulbous trunk conceals a cavernously hollow interior. Please treat it with the utmost respect. Join the road by Seathwaite Bridge and continue over Seatoller Bridge to finally turn left at the junction.

WALK 29 FACT FILE

START & FINISH: SEATOLLER CAR PARK (245138)

MAPS: OS L89 OR OL4

ACCESS: FOLLOW THE B5289

BORROWDALE ROAD TO KESWICK

WATERING HOLES: CAFES AT SEATOLLER AND SEATHWAITE

LENGTH: 5.5KM

TIME: 2½ HOURS

DIFFICULTY: EASY; LEVEL GOING INCLUDING A SHORT ROAD SECTION

CASTLE CRAG RISING FROM THE JAWS OF BORROWDALE

River Derwent, New Bridge, Jaws of Borrowdale, Hows Woods, Castle Crag

Low Hows Wood

INTRODUCTION

10KM WEST OF KESWICK. WITHIN THE 'JAWS OF BORROWDALE' THE ANCIENT CELTIC STRONGHOLD OF CASTLE CRAG RISES FROM SYLVAN SPLENDOUR AND THE CRYSTAL-CLEAR WATERS OF THE RIVER DERWENT TO TAKE A COMMANDING POSITION OVER BEAUTIFUL BORROWDALE. THIS ROUTE CIRCUMNAVIGATES THE CRAGGY OUTCROP BEFORE ASCENDING TO ITS SUMMIT.

STEP BY STEP

▲ Bear right along the road past Rosthwaite village hall, until a cobbled track leads right through the stone buildings to gain a lane. Continue along the lane to meet the green crystal waters of the tree-lined River Derwent. Follow the lane along the river bank before crossing the stone arch of New Bridge. Follow the west bank of the river to pass a rocky knoll bedecked with fine oaks. Continue, to enter the lovely mixed deciduous woods of High Hows.

▲ Follow the signed path to rise a little before bearing right. Slight descent brings the river to view again and a track through the woods of Low Hows leads to a gate atop a little rise. Below this, above the wide and open bend in the river, a track breaks off ascending to the left. Follow this track to cross a tiny footbridge and rise to quit the wood via a gate. The stone track and rocky steps traverse beneath the steep west face of the crag before a cairn marks a path leading off to the left.

New Bridge over the River Derwent

On the summit of Castle Crag

Castle Crag

Take this path, climbing the west flank of the hill until a ladder stile leads by Scots pine onto the bank of a long abandoned slate quarry. Trending right follow the old quarrymen's zigzag path up the slate to gain the level north col of Castle Crag. Expansive view south over upper Borrowdale. Climb the nose following the zigzags until a quarry opens on the left. Take the worn path ascending through larch to the right of this. Care – the edges of the quarry are unfenced and another quarry hole lies just to the right of the path. Emerge onto the level summit plateau. Observe magnificent aspect over Derwent Water to mighty Skiddaw and the ancient earthwork mound running around the summit rim. The summit lies atop the rocky knoll adorned with commemorative plaque.

Retrace steps to the north col and continue to descend to find a ladder stile leading north over the stone wall. Follow the steepening path down the east flank, continue through woods, to regain the original track by the River Derwent. Bear right to Rosthwaite.

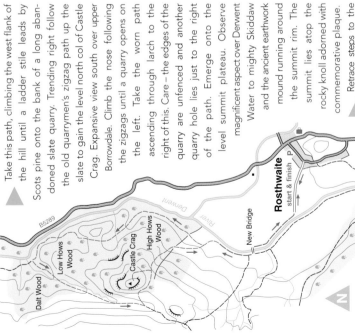

Dalt Wood
Low Hows Wood
Castle Crag
High Hows Wood
B5289
River Derwent
Rosthwaite
start & finish P
New Bridge

1 kilometre

N

WALK 30 FACT FILE

LENGTH: 6KM

TIME: 2 HOURS

DIFFICULTY: DIFFICULT, STRENUOUS ASCENT AND DESCENT, BEWARE OF EXPOSED UNFENCED QUARRY FACES AND CRAGS

START & FINISH: ROSTHWAITE VILLAGE CAR PARKS (257148)

MAPS: OS L90 OR OL4

ACCESS: FROM KESWICK DRIVE DOWN THE BORROWDALE VALLEY ALONG THE B5289 FOR 10KM TO THE VILLAGE OF ROSTHWAITE AND TURN RIGHT TO FIND TWO CAR PARKS (NATIONAL TRUST AND VILLAGE HALL)

WATERING HOLES: SCAFELL HOTEL AND A CAFE IN ROSTHWAITE

DERWENTWATER HEIGHTS: BY CASTLERIGG TO WALLA CRAG

Castle Head, Springs Wood, Castlerigg, Walla Crag, Cat Gill, Great Wood, Calfclose Bay, Friar's Crag

Derwent Water

INTRODUCTION

KESWICK. THE NORTHERN HEAD OF DERWENT WATER OPENS TO KESWICK AND THE NORTHERN FELLS TO STUNNING EFFECT. SAVOURING THE MYRIAD, TREE-FRINGED DELIGHTS OF THE LAKE AND EXPLORING THE COUNTRYSIDE BEYOND, THIS CLOCKWISE ROUND RISING TO WALLA CRAG ALSO OFFERS WONDERFUL PANORAMAS OF THE SURROUNDING FELLS.

STEP BY STEP

There may be a prettier lake than Derwent Water, with its jewelled expanse fringed by oakwoods, crag and fell, though after this walk you could be forgiven for doubting it. At Derwent Bay take the path left into Cockshott Wood opposite the landing stages. Follow through the wood to exit by a lane which leads across the fields. Cross the road and climb the steps into Castlehead Wood. Follow the main path, bearing left to make a circumnavigatory ascent, before a path climbs to the right to crest the rocky knoll of Castle Head.

Descend to the main path then bear right to a kissing gate which leads to a lane. Continue to Springs Road and bear right, ascending to cross a bridge opposite Springs Farm. Take the track up through the wood. Go right at the junction then follow up the edge of the wood. Continue in ascent until a footbridge crosses left to Castlerigg Road. Bear right and continue to its end to recross the stream by footbridge.

The path leads up by the wall, crosses a stile, and out onto the open shoulder of the fell. Ascend the steep grassy nose. The going levels until a stile on the right, through the fenceline, leads to a path which follows the edge of the crag. Those wishing to stay away from the cliff edge may take

View from Walla Crag

74

a higher stile. Follow the path which crosses the head of a gully, Lady's Rake, to climb onto the polished rock cap of Walla Crag. Stunning views.

Return to the boundary and follow down the wall, taking the lower stile. The path descends steeply above the tumbling waters of Cat Gill to meet a track by a bridge, before bearing right into Great Wood. Follow this until a descent leads into the car park. Pass straight across, to find a path which descends to a gap in the wall by the Borrowdale road. Take the gap in the wall opposite, and follow the path to the lakeshore.

On Walla Crag

Bear right following around Calfclose Bay, by Stable Hills, around Ings Wood and Strandshag Bay to the stand of Scots pine on Friar's Crag. Easily back to Derwent Head.

Friar's Crag, Derwent Water

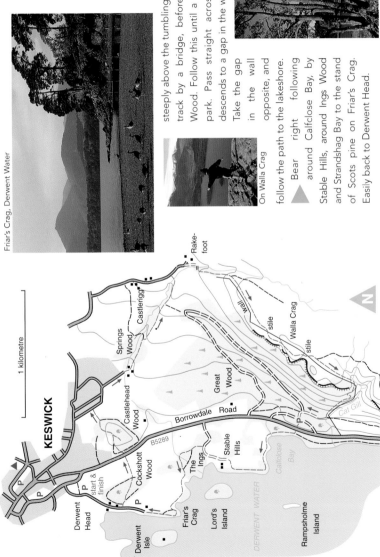

By Derwent Water, Calfclose Bay

1 kilometre

KESWICK

Derwent Head

Derwent Isle

Friar's Crag

Lord's Island

Cockshott Wood

The Ings.

Castlehead Wood

Springs Wood

Castlerigg

Rakefoot

B5289

start & finish

Stable Hills

Borrowdale Road

Great Wood

wall

stile

Walla Crag

stile

stile

Cat Gill

Calfclose Bay

DERWENT WATER

Rampsholme Island

N

WALK 31 FACT FILE

START & FINISH: DERWENT HEAD CAR PARK (265229)

MAPS: OS L89 OR OL4

ACCESS: SIGNED FROM KESWICK

WATERING HOLES: CAFES BY DERWENT HEAD BAY

LENGTH: 8.5KM

TIME: 3 HOURS

DIFFICULTY: MODERATE; GOOD PATHS THOUGH WITH STEEP ASCENT AND DESCENT

LATRIGG ABOVE KESWICK

Spooney Green Lane, Ewe How, Birkett Wood, Millen Dodd, Latrigg, Brundholme Wood, Whinney Brow

Latrigg

INTRODUCTION

KESWICK. ATTACHED TO THE GREAT SKIDDAW MASSIF YET INDEPENDENT IN SPIRIT, LATRIGG OCCUPIES DOMINANT POSITION ABOVE KESWICK. THIS ROUTE CLIMBS TO THE SUMMIT BEFORE FALLING DOWN THE LONG EASTERN SHOULDER TO FINALLY TRAVERSE UNSUSPECTED TRACK AND PATH TO MAKE RETURN ACROSS THE FACE OF THE HILL.

On Latrigg with Skiddaw beyond

STEP BY STEP

▲ Sugar Mountain – Rio de Janeiro. Table Mountain – Cape Town. Latrigg – Keswick. Those who think they know Latrigg by casual observation from Keswick will be pleasantly surprised by the hidden interest of this route. Climb Spooney Green Lane taking the bridge across the throbbing bypass. Continue to pass the woods beneath Whinney Brow. Follow the track in ascent, to pass Ewe How, Round How and Birkett Wood, until, with forestry below, a green track zigzags off to the right.

▲ Ascend with this when, at the highest stone gateless gatestoop, the track bears off right. Making gentle ascent traverse Mallen Dodd to a bench and very fine position above Keswick town. Derwent Water and Borrowdale lie beyond. Skiddaw rises majestically behind. The Dodds and Helvellyn stretch to the east.

The grassy track zigzags back to the left, making final ascent to the highest point before carrying along by the raised bank which runs along the rim of Latrigg. Cross the stile before falling slightly left down the shoulder to gain a track above the wood. Follow the track until, at a point where it steepens, and a little way before it falls to intercept a surfaced road, a grassy track signed 'Permitted Woodland Walk Keswick' leads sharply off right.

Take this track, traversing above the trees of Brundholme Wood. Continue along the path, dropping down into the

woods for a short way, only to climb again to follow a lesser track. Keep along this, with a few undulations, traversing the thickly wooded hillside to emerge into the open beneath Whinney Brow. Large sweet-chestnut trees and Scots pine above. Keep right at the junction and descend left to cross a track and intercept a further track at a lower level. Follow this to the right to emerge by gate onto Spooney Green Lane.

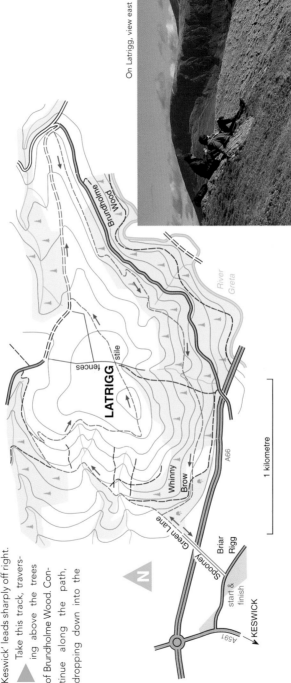

On Latrigg, view east

1 kilometre

River Greta

LATRIGG

fences

stile

Whinny Brow

Brundholme Wood

A66

Spooney Green Lane

Briar Rigg

start & finish

KESWICK

A591

N

W A L K   3 2   F A C T   F I L E

LENGTH: 8KM

TIME: 3 HOURS

DIFFICULTY: MODERATE; STRENUOUS ASCENT, MEANDERING DESCENT

START & FINISH: BRIAR RIGG, PARKING BY ROAD (268241)

MAPS: OS L90 OR OL4

ACCESS: ON THE NORTHERN EDGE OF KESWICK

WATERING HOLES: NONE EN ROUTE, PLENTIFUL IN KESWICK

CASTLERIGG STONE CIRCLE TO LOW NADDLE FELL

High Nest, Nest Brow, St John's Chapel, Low Naddle Fell, Tewet Tarn, Naddle Bridge, Goosewell Farm

INTRODUCTION

2KM EAST OF KESWICK. BENEATH HIGH AND DRAMATIC FELLS, ON AN ELEVATED SHOULDER LOOKING OVER A MAJOR MEETING OF WAYS, CASTLERIGG IS UNDOUBTEDLY LAKELAND'S GRANDEST STONE CIRCLE. THIS WALK DIPS OVER THE NADDLE VALLEY, THEN RISES TO ST JOHN'S, TO TRAVERSE LOW NADDLE FELL TO TEWIT TARN BEFORE MAKING RETURN.

INTRODUCTION

Castlerigg Stone Circle

STEP BY STEP

A timelessly impressive backdrop to this walk whichever way you turn. Mighty Blencathra and Skiddaw to the north, Grisedale Pike and the north-western fells to the west, Castlerigg Fell to the south and the Dodds and Helvellyn to the east. The Neolithic stone circle of Castlerigg (circa 2,500BC) could hardly fail to make a huge impression.

A little gate leads to the circle and a viewpoint east over Naddle Valley. Return to the road, bear right, then right again in 200m to follow the path across the fields to the house known as High Nest. Pass through the buildings and down the lane until, at a cattle grid, the path bears off left to join a lower lane. Go right to the main road joining it on Nest Brow hill. Keep left to find a stile through the wall in 50m.

Follow the path down through the fields. Cross a little bridge and bear left in the valley bottom. Cross the gated bridge over the clear

Towards Low Naddle Fell from Nest Brow

To St Johns

waters of Naddle Beck, continuing past a little wood to bear right across a field. After a way, a sign points left and this is followed to a kissing gate which leads to rougher fellside. The path leads to an exit onto a stony track. Continue over the brow of the hill to little St John's Chapel. Rebuilt 1845 and little changed since, it gives its name to the next vale below.

The stile opposite leads to a path beneath a crag and over a stone wall to cross Low Naddle Fell. Descent passes east of forlorn Tewet Tarn to join the road (old A66). Go left and left again at the junction (older A66) to cross Naddle Bridge. A path leads left off the road. At the divergence of ways go left through a gate to make a diagonal crossing over the field, ascending gently (right of way though poorly defined) directly to Goosewell Farm. Left up the road.

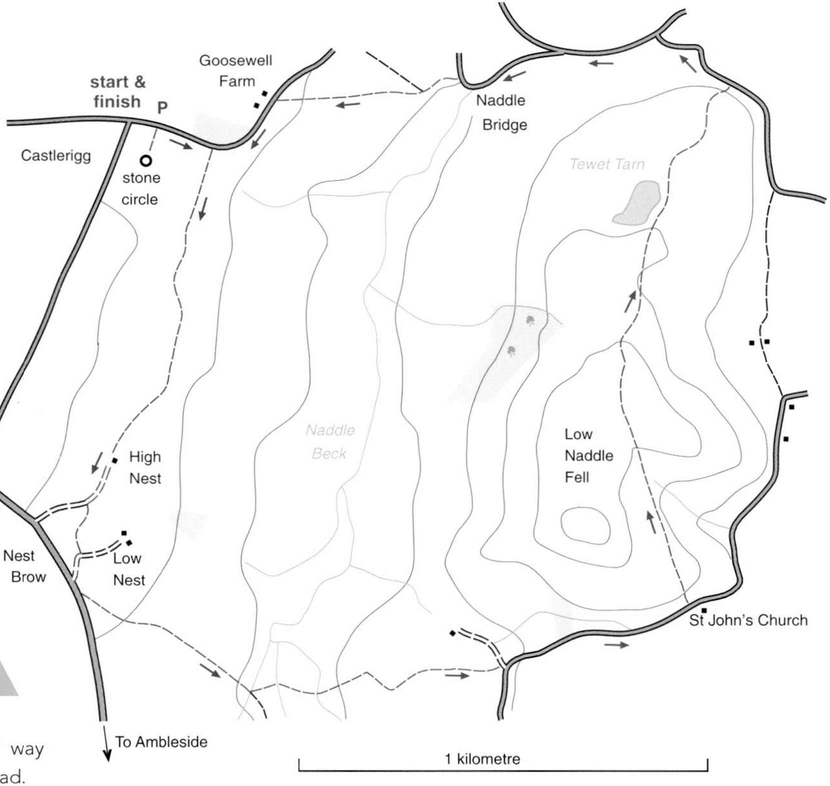

WALK 33 FACT FILE

START & FINISH: PARKING OPPOSITE CASTLERIGG STONE CIRCLE (292236)

MAPS: OS L90 OR OL4

ACCESS: TAKE THE HIGH FIELDSIDE LANE ABOVE KESWICK

WATERING HOLES: NONE EN ROUTE, PLENTIFUL IN KESWICK

LENGTH: 6.5KM

TIME: 2½ HOURS

DIFFICULTY: MODERATE; INCLUDES SHORT ASCENT AND EASY OPEN FELL

HARROP TARN AMONGST THE WYTHBURN FELLS

Dob Gill, Thirlmere Conifers, Harrop Tarn, Mosshause Gill, Swithin Crag, Bank Crags

INTRODUCTION

13KM NORTH OF AMBLESIDE. SHROUDED BY THIRLMERE'S DARK CONIFERS HARROP TARN RESTS HIDDEN IN ITS GLACIAL BASIN HIGH ABOVE THE SOUTH-EAST END OF THE RESERVOIR. THIS CLOCKWISE ROUND RISES STEEPLY BY DOB GILL TO VISIT THE TARN BEFORE UTILISING FOREST TRACKS TO FACILITATE RETURN.

INTRODUCTION

The forest track to Harrop Tarn

STEP BY STEP

▲ Long, narrow and moody Thirlmere Reservoir runs due north between the great Helvellyn Massif. With its fringe of conifers it more resembles a dark Scottish loch than anything Lakeland. Below the car park, when the reservoir is low, the drowned community of Wythburn, flooded in 1894, reappears. A visit is recommended.

▲ Steps at the back of the car park lead to a zigzag path which climbs steeply through the conifers, occasional beech and crag, to overlook the tumbling waterfalls of Dob Gill. The path levels and leads to the point at which Dob Gill flows from the tarn.

▲ Bear right (a bridge or ford leads left over the beck to allow a better view of the tarn) and continue along the forest track with occasional glimpses of the tarn through the trees. The track rises by little Mosshause Beck to a junction. Go right and follow this track to the gate leaving the conifers. A recent clearing of pine allows an excursion out right to the viewpoint of Swithin Crag. Excellent vantage over the reservoir and the Helvellyn Massif, with the drawback of being boggy and rough with forest debris.

Harrop Tarn

Dob Gill

A path leads right, off the track, down the open hillside, to pass a curious wrought-iron circular fence, perhaps once an old well. Follow an old walled track past the elegant Scots pine and on to the road. Bear right. Incidentally the alien conifers shouldn't really be here. Thankfully, the existing Water Authority does seem to be thinning them and replacing with broad-leaved trees.

Helvellyn Massif viewed from the west overlooking the hollow of Harrop Tarn

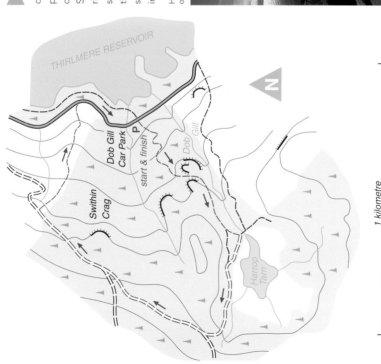

THIRLMERE RESERVOIR

Dob Gill
Car Park

start & finish

Dob Gill

Swithin
Crag

Harrop
Tarn

N

1 kilometre

WALK 34 FACT FILE

LENGTH: 2.5KM

TIME: 1½ HOURS

DIFFICULTY: MODERATE; STEEP INITIAL ASCENT

START & FINISH: DOBGILL CAR PARK (316141)

MAPS: OS L90 OR OL5

ACCESS: FROM AMBLESIDE FOLLOW THE A591 NORTH OVER DUNMAIL RAISE TO TURN LEFT AT THE END OF THIRLMERE RESERVOIR

WATERING HOLES: NONE EN ROUTE, KING'S HEAD HOTEL AT THIRLSPOT NEARBY

BY RUTHWAITE AND ULDALE TO ROUND OVER WATER

John Peel Cottage, Uldale, Stanthwaite, Chapelhouse Dam, Orthwaite Hall, Roman Camp, Overwater Hall

INTRODUCTION
17KM NORTH OF KESWICK, OVER WATER RESTS IN
THE GREEN BASIN BETWEEN THE NORTHERN FELLS
AND BINSEY, AT THE VERY NORTHERN EDGE OF THE
NATIONAL PARK. THIS CLOCKWISE ROUND MAKES A
WIDE CIRCUMNAVIGATION OF THE TARN TO ENJOY
THE REGION'S UNIQUE ATMOSPHERE WHILE INCLUDING
NUMEROUS FEATURES OF INTEREST ON THE WAY.
INTRODUCTION

Chapelhouse Reservoir

STEP BY STEP

Not very long ago the stirring strains of 'Do you ken John Peel?' rang out from every school and pub in Lakeland. This was his country. He lived in a cottage at Ruthwaite and used to hunt astride his pony Binsey. Pass through the village and bear right, opposite 'John Peel Cottage', to follow a path across the field. In 100m bear left, down the hill, to follow a muddy path (way-marked) and cross a track to gain a narrow foot-bridge over Ruthwaite Beck.

A grassy path leads by the boundary hedge, over a number of stiles, to emerge onto the surfaced road. Go left, bridge over River Ellen, and continue to Uldale.

Turn right in the centre of the village up the hill to pass the old school at the brow, before continuing down through the buildings of Stanthwaite to Stanthwaite Bridge.

Go left immediately and cross the fields, marked by distant posts, to emerge onto a lane. Turn left. Pass Chapel House Farm and on over the dam of Chapelhouse Reservoir to climb to the surfaced road. Go right, passing the reservoir and Over Water, to reach the grand old buildings of

82

North-west across Over Water to Binsey

Orthwaite Hall. A stile over the wall leads right down through the fields, over a little bridge and by a fir plantation, to pass the unmistakable bank-and-ditch structure of a Roman encampment.

Bear right, then left, to cross the flat bridge and over the field to Overwater Hall. A slightly odd, leaning pole-like object proves, on closer examination, to be even more curious than first impressions suggest – the 'stone man with hat' of Orthwaite Hall. Could it be John Peel himself? Keep right to pass the hall and up the lane. Cross the road to continue via a grand avenue of trees. Keep on over the hill to the next road and cross directly to follow a (vague) path through the field and up to the Ruthwaite road beneath Binsey fell.

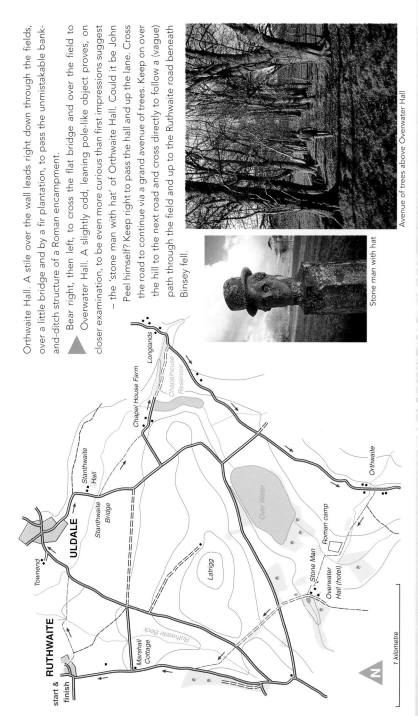

Stone man with hat

Avenue of trees above Overwater Hall

WALK 35 FACT FILE

START & FINISH: GRASS VERGE OPPOSITE THE VILLAGE OF RUTHWAITE

MAPS: OS L90 OR OL4

ACCESS: FROM KESWICK HEAD NORTH ON THE A591 UNTIL AT KILNHILL A MINOR ROAD HEADS OFF RIGHT TO RUTHWAITE (237367)

WATERING HOLES: SNOOTY FOX INN AT ULDALE

LENGTH: 9.5KM

TIME: 3 HOURS

DIFFICULTY: MODERATE; BOGGY IN PLACES, ROUTE FINDING REQUIRES CARE

Longlands

Chapel House Farm

Chapelhouse Reservoir

Stanthwaite Hall

ULDALE

Stanthwaite Bridge

Townend

RUTHWAITE

start & finish

Marshall Cottage

Ruthwaite Beck

Latrigg

Over Water

Orthwaite

Roman camp

Stone Man

Overwater Hall (hotel)

N

1 kilometre

HIGH BOWSCALE TARN IN THE NORTHERN FELLS

Drycomb, Bowscale Tarn, River Caldew, Roundhouse, Mosedale, Mosedale Bridge

Looking up Mosedale to Roundhouse

INTRODUCTION

16KM NORTH-EAST OF KESWICK. HIDDEN AMONGST
THE FAR NORTHERN FELLS ABOVE THE MOSEDALE
VALLEY, AND OPPOSITE THE ANCIENT HILL FORT OF
CARROCK FELL, LONELY AND WILD, SITS LITTLE
BOWSCALE TARN. THIS CIRCUIT FOLLOWS A TRACK
WHICH MAKES GRADUAL RISE TO THE TARN FOLLOWED
BY RAPID DESCENT AND LEVEL RETURN ALONG
THE MOSEDALE VALLEY.

STEP BY STEP

There is a quiet power in these untamed far-flung Northern Fells. They offer strategic position above the plains of Eden, as witnessed by the Iron Age hill fort which garlands the top of Carrock Fell, once the fabled stronghold of Boadicea. Within their depths too, is incredible wealth. Wolfram and scheelite, the ores of tungsten, were mined as recently as the 1980s at nearby Carrock Mine. Now the mines are silent and the immortal fish of Bowscale Tarn, possibly Arctic char, noted by Wordworth in his poem 'Song at the Feast of Brougham Castle', can go about their business relatively undisturbed.

Just above the cottages at Bowscale, through a gate and kissing gate, a track traverses the hillside above the Mosedale Valley and the River

Bowscale Tarn

84

Caldew, to make a gradual ascent to the tarn. Easy going, it nevertheless imparts a strong feeling of climbing into wild hills. Near the top, bear right beneath the shielding barrier of glacial moraine, to arrive at the point at which Tarn Syke beck exits.

In descent keep well left (east) of the little beck. Aim for the Roundhouse, charmingly situated by the bank of the River Caldew far

below. Its distinctive shape makes it easy to recognise, even from this altitude. After a little way a grassy track appears to make pleasant zigzag descent. A footbridge crosses the river to pass the barns dated 1702, and leads to the road. Go right to Mosedale noting the 'Friends' Meeting House 1702', to turn right again and on over Mosedale Bridge back to Bowscale.

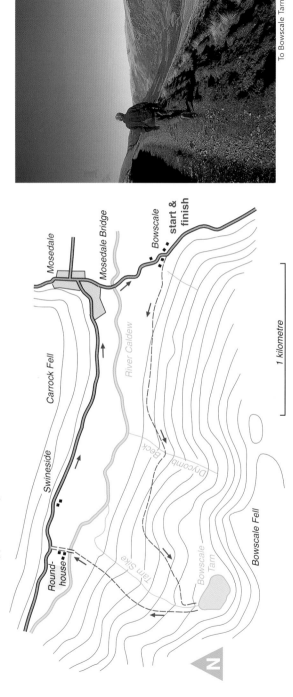

To Bowscale Tarn

WALK 36 FACT FILE

LENGTH: 7KM

TIME: 2½ HOURS

DIFFICULTY: MODERATE; GRADUAL ASCENT, STEEP THOUGH STRAIGHTFORWARD DESCENT

START & FINISH: PARKING BY HAMLET OF BOWSCALE (359316)

MAPS: OS L90 OR OL5

ACCESS: FOLLOW THE A66 EAST FROM KESWICK TO TURN LEFT ON THE MINOR ROAD (TO CALDBECK) WHICH LEADS THROUGH MUNGRISDALE NEARBY

WATERING HOLES: NONE EN ROUTE, THE MILL INN AT MUNGRISDALE NEARBY

POOLEY BRIDGE TO HEUGHSCAR HILL BY WAY OF MOOR DIVOCK

Roehead, High Street Roman Road, The Cockpit, Ketley Gate, Moor Divock, Heughscar Hill

Roe House

INTRODUCTION

9KM SOUTH-WEST OF PENRITH. MARKING THE
NORTHERN TERMINUS OF THE GREAT HIGH STREET
ROMAN ROAD, HEUGHSCAR HILL STANDS ABOVE
POOLEY BRIDGE AT THE END OF ULLSWATER.
OFFERING OPEN VIEWS OVER ULLSWATER TO THE
FELLS AND OUT OVER THE PLAINS BEYOND, THIS
ROUND MAKES APPROACH VIA THE ANTIQUITIES
OF MOOR DIVOCK.

STEP BY STEP

▲ Head down the main street away from the bridge to turn right by the church. Ascend the road, continuing straight across at the junction, to join a track at the road's end by Roe House. Climb the track continuing to a point where the going levels and the track intercepts the route of High Street Roman road (signed).

▲ Bear right along the boggy Roman road to reach a low circular ancient wall of earth and stone. This, the Cockpit, is the largest of the many prehistoric antiquities to be found on Moor Divock.

▲ A way leads back diagonally north by the shallow Shake Holes to the original track at Ketley Gate. (A little to the right the White Raise burial cairn is worthy of attention.) Either follow the track which leads north to the walled wood and bear left to find the top of Heughscar Hill, or go left up a well-worn path through the bracken, starting by the stone parish-boundary marker. A commanding viewpoint.

Track from Pooley Bridge looking over Ullswater

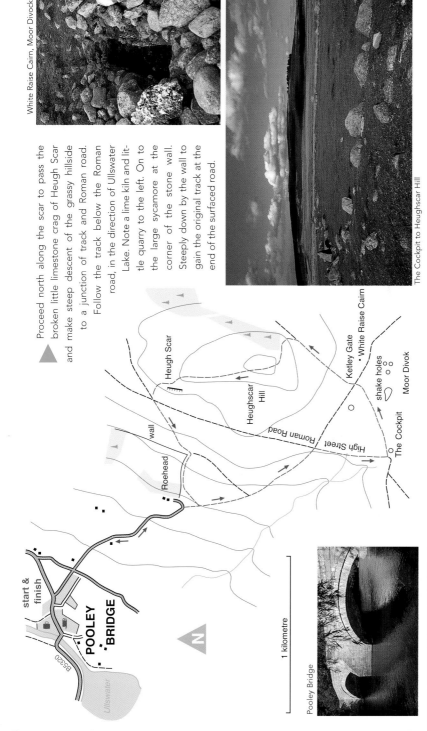

White Raise Cairn, Moor Divock

Proceed north along the scar to pass the broken little limestone crag of Heugh Scar and make steep descent of the grassy hillside to a junction of track and Roman road. Follow the track below the Roman road, in the direction of Ullswater Lake. Note a lime kiln and little quarry to the left. On to the large sycamore at the corner of the stone wall. Steeply down by the wall to gain the original track at the end of the surfaced road.

The Cockpit to Heughscar Hill

Heugh Scar

Heughscar Hill

Roman Road

High Street

Ketley Gate

White Raise Cairn

shake holes

Moor Divock

The Cockpit

wall

Roehead

start & finish

POOLEY BRIDGE

Ullswater

B5320

N

1 kilometre

Pooley Bridge

WALK 37 FACT FILE

START & FINISH: POOLEY BRIDGE (470244)

MAPS: OS L90 OR OL5

ACCESS: LEAVE PENRITH SOUTH ON THE A6 TO TURN RIGHT ON THE B5320

WATERING HOLES: NUMEROUS INNS AND CAFES IN POOLEY BRIDGE

LENGTH: 7.5KM

TIME: 2½ HOURS

DIFFICULTY: MODERATE; STRAIGHTFORWARD ASCENT AND DESCENT

PATTERDALE TO HOWTOWN: A TRAVERSE OF ULLSWATER'S SOUTH SHORE

Patterdale, Side Farm, Silver Crag, Scalehow Force, Sandwick, Hallinhag Wood, Howtown Wyke

INTRODUCTION

20KM SOUTH-WEST OF PENRITH. BELOW STEEP FELLS, ON PATH AND TRACK, BY OAK, SILVER BIRCH, FERN AND GORSE. THE RADIANT BEAUTY AND SYLVAN SERENITY OF LAKE ULLSWATER ARE ENCOMPASSED ON THIS OUTSTANDING WALK. A LINEAR OUTING, ROUNDING THE HEAD OF ULLSWATER AND CONTINUING TO HOWTOWN TO MAKE RETURN BY STEAMER.

Over Ullswater to south shore and Sandwick Bay

STEP BY STEP

With its head and south shore dominated by steep fells, the three legs of Ullswater lead north eastwards from the central fells to the open plains beyond. This walk rounds the head of the lake before following the south shore along its middle leg, to offer a walk of outstanding natural beauty. Return by steamer is part of the fun of the outing. Regular sailings occur daily during the summer months - though a timetable should be obtained in Glenridding first!

▲ From Glenridding follow the road to Patterdale. Turn left along the lane which leads to Side Farm. Follow the track left until a signed path rises, by the larch trees, to the right. (With less of a climb, an alternative route keeps along the original track to round Silver Point at a lower level.) Join a higher grassy track and go left to follow it into the little corridor behind Silver Crag. A rough scramble up the crag is rewarded by an outstanding view along the first two legs of the lake.

Over Ullswater to south shore below Place Fell

88

Down the path, to a junction with the lower path from Silver Point, and continue above the shore until, at Roscombe Rigg, the path moves away from the lake above Scalehow Wood. Cross the footbridge over Scalehow Beck (waterfall above best viewed beyond the bridge), and continue along the track to the hamlet of Sandwick. Go left, then right, to cross the bridge over Sandwick Beck.

Continue, to gain and traverse the shoreline by the oaks of Hallinhag Wood. The path rounds the headland of Hallin Fell to continue above Howtown Wyke Bay to the buildings of Waternook. Bear left down to the shore and continue directly to the steamer pier.

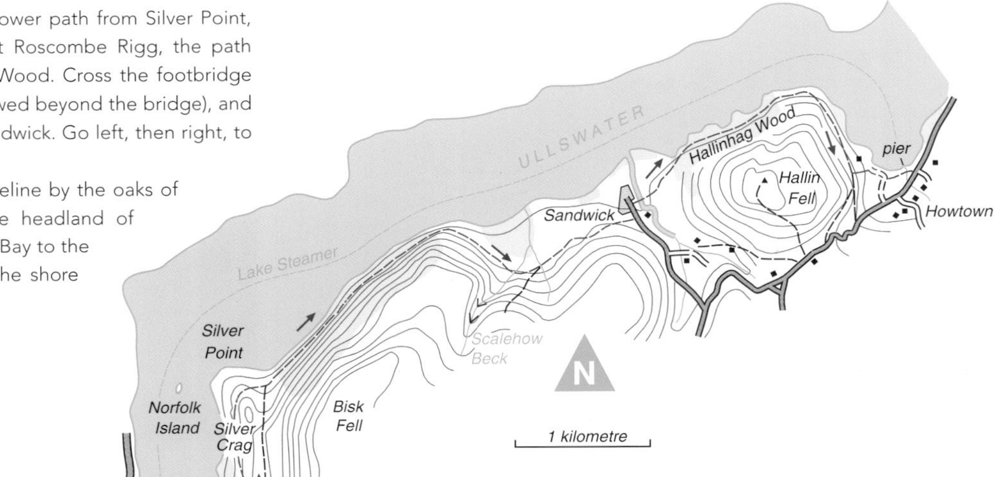

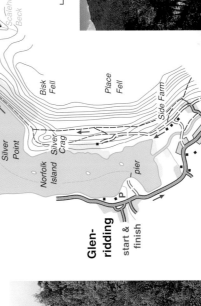
Ullswater steamer arrives at Howtown

1 kilometre

Scalehow Force

WALK 38 FACT FILE

(386170)

LENGTH: 10KM

TIME: 3½ HOURS

DIFFICULTY: EASY

START & FINISH: GLENRIDDING

MAPS: OS L90 OR OL5

ACCESS: FROM PENRITH FOLLOW THE A66 THEN HEAD LEFT ALONG THE A692

WATERING HOLES: HOWTOWN HOTEL AT THE END OF THE WALK

Map labels: Howtown, pier, Hallinhag Wood, Hallin Fell, ULLSWATER, Sandwick, Scalehow Beck, N, Lake Steamer, Silver Point, Norfolk Island, Silver Crag, Bisk Fell, Place Fell, Side Farm, Patterdale, Glen-ridding, start & finish, P, pier

A CROSSING OF GRISEDALE AT THE HEAD OF ULLSWATER

Patterdale Hotel, Thornhow, Grisedale Beck, Lanty's Tarn, Westside, Glenridding, Ullswater

INTRODUCTION

21KM SOUTH-WEST OF PENRITH. THIS PARTICULAR GRISEDALE IS THE IMPRESSIVE MOUNTAIN VALLEY WHICH FALLS TO THE HEAD OF ULLSWATER BENEATH ST SUNDAY CRAG AND THE PRECIPITOUS EAST FACE OF THE HELVELLYN MASSIF. A CLOCKWISE ROUND EXPLORES THE FOOT OF THE DALE BEFORE MAKING RETURN VIA THE HEAD OF ULLSWATER.

Over Grisedale

STEP BY STEP

▲ Pass the Ullswater end of the Patterdale Hotel to find a little path which leads right through the cluster of birch to a kissing gate. An open track rises rightwards to traverse the hillside above the stone wall. Open views extend over Ullswater, and there are many fine trees with a mixture of apple and thorn blossom at spring-time.

▲ Pass through a gate and keep along the well-defined track. Cross the stepping stones over Hag Beck, to contour around the hillside and enter a wood of tall ancient larch. Continue, until some little stone enclosures stand against the hillside to the left and a kissing gate on the right leads down through the fields to the old stone barns of Thornhow. Follow down the track, bear right and then left along the surfaced road, to cross the fine stone-arch bridge over Grisedale Beck.

▲ Climb the lane, keeping left at the junction, to emerge through the fell wall. Go right along the level grassy track for 100m then climb steeply leftwards to skirt the reclusive Lanty's Tarn. Beyond the tarn a path

Head of Ullswater

Glenridding

St Patrick's Well

Westside

Keldas

Lanty's Tarn

Ullswater

A592

Hag Beck

Thorn-how

Patterdale

Hotel

start & finish

P

N

1 kilometre

leads down the hillside, eventually falling to the buildings of Westside. However, a worthwhile diversion can first be made by turning right, beyond the kissing gate which leaves the tarn, to follow the path to the summit of Keldas. A short steep ascent is rewarded by very fine views over Ullswater.

Returning to the original path continue the descent to pass Westside and on to the banks of Glenridding Beck. Bear right to reach main road in Glenridding. Follow the road to Patterdale. By the lake a permissive path keeps right above the road and St Patrick's Well only to rejoin the road and cross to the other side to divert through the trees for a short way.

Thornhow, Grisedale

Lanty's Tarn

WALK 39 FACT FILE

START & FINISH: PATTERDALE HOTEL (396159)

MAPS: OS L90 OR OL5

ACCESS: FROM PENRITH FOLLOW THE A66 THEN HEAD LEFT ALONG THE A692

WATERING HOLES: PLENTIFUL IN BOTH GLENRIDDING AND PATTERDALE

LENGTH: 5KM

TIME: 2½ HOURS

DIFFICULTY: MODERATE; A SHORT STRENUOUS ASCENT, BOGGY IN PLACES

MARDALE'S COFFIN ROAD FROM HAWESWATER TO SWINDALE

Mardale Head, Old Corpse Road, Swindale Head, Hobgrumble Gill Falls, Mosedale Cottage, Gatescarth Pass

Above Haweswater

INTRODUCTION

32KM SOUTH-WEST OF PENRITH. ISOLATED BY HIGH FELL AND DESOLATE MOOR, THE VALLEYS OF DROWNED MARDALE (HAWESWATER RESERVOIR), MOSEDALE LEADING TO SWINDALE, AND LONGSLEDDALE RADIATE TO THE EASTERN FRINGES OF THE NATIONAL PARK. THIS WALK ON THE WILD SIDE CONNECTS THESE LARGELY FORGOTTEN DALES BY THE OLD CORPSE ROAD AND GATESCARTH PASS.

STEP BY STEP

▲ A remote outing in a mountain area, which should not be underestimated, particularly if tackled in winter. The drowning of Mardale and the annexing of Swindale by the-then Manchester Water Authority has at least kept this eastern area of the Lake District quiet and untamed. The golden eagle, peregrine falcon, red fox and red deer reign relatively freely here.

▲ Walk down the road (or follow lakeshore path to same point) until the Old Corpse Road to Swindale makes steep zigzag ascent up the hillside to the right. The drowned community of Mardale, the church and Dun Bull Inn, all lie beneath the waters below except in times of drought. Pass the deserted stone buildings by the track and continue over the moor, dropping gently to the farm of Swindale Head.

▲ Bear right and follow the track, with the rocky knoll of the Knott to the left and the long tumbling waterfalls of Hobgrumble Gill to the right.

To Mardale Head from Old Corpse Road

92

The Knot, Swindale

Follow the path which rises into the valley of Mosedale, and continue up to wade a stream before reaching the lonely deserted Mosedale Cottage. Once of service to quarrymen and farmers it now acts as a bothy for walkers – if you use it please keep it clean.

Keep along the path/track rising to a gate through the fence on the col – very boggy. Descend the track, keeping low should there be a choice, to intercept the packhorse route which rises from Longsleddale at Brownhowe Bottom. There are numerous slate quarries nearby. The valley of Longsleddale takes its name from the fact that it was a long way for the quarrymen to sled out their slates. Very boggy in places. Bear right and follow up the track to crest the summit of Gatescarth Pass (believe it or not officially still classed as a road). Long, though pleasant and easier descent, leads back to Mardale Head.

Meeting of ways at Brownhowe Bottom

The map shows the route with labels: Swindale Head, The Knot, Old Corpse Road, HAWESWATER, The Rigg, start & finish P, Mardale Head, Harter Fell, Adam Seat, Gatescarth Pass, Branstree, Brownhowe Bottom, Mosedale Cottage, Selside Pike, Hobgrumble Gill, Falls, Mosedale Beck, Mosedale, N, 1 kilometre

WALK 40 FACT FILE

START & FINISH: MARDALE HEAD CAR PARK AT THE HEAD OF HAWESWATER (469107)

MAPS: OS L90 OR OL5/7

ACCESS: FROM PENRITH GO SOUTH ALONG THE A6 TO SHAP. FROM HERE A MINOR ROAD LEADS TO BAMPTON AND CONTINUES TO FOLLOW HAWESWATER

WATERING HOLES: NONE EN ROUTE; ST PATRICK'S WELL INN AT BAMPTON NEARBY

LENGTH: 14KM

TIME: 5 HOURS

DIFFICULTY: DIFFICULT; REMOTE, THREE SECTIONS OF SUSTAINED ASCENT, ROUGH AND BOGGY IN PLACES

I've long wanted to write and photograph this guidebook and many elements have finally come together to make it possible. I would personally like to thank the team at David & Charles, particularly Sue Viccars who brought the concept to fruition and art editor Sue Cleave who turned my requirements into practicable reality.

Similarly thanks must go to Martin Bagness, of Orienteering Services, whose knowledge of the complex terrain and ability to rationalise it into an attractive and straightforward map are, I believe, unsurpassed.

For accompanying me on many a walk, and locating themselves strategically as required, a special thanks to my family: my wife and first-draft editor, Susan, my daughter Rowan and my son William.

I am indebted to a great number of people for assisting me in this project, including those who walked the walks with me, became a part of my photographic imagery, shared their knowledge, corrected text and supported me personally:

Dave Birkett, Marian and Peter Cheung, Ann and Jackson Corrie, Brian and June Dodson, John Hargreaves, Alan Hinkes, Outdoor Writers Guild, Jon Rigby, Jenny Siddall, Andrew and Eszter Sheehan, Kyla Spady, Jo Squires, John White. For local knowledge and pronunciation thanks to Andrew, Ed, George, John, and Maureen Birkett, Melly and Marie Dixon, Jackie and Mark Dugdale. There were many more and I must offer my sincere apologies to those whose names I have missed.

Credit must also be given to those who keep a watchful eye over the Lake District and do a tremendous job preserving its beauty and character: the Lake District National Park Authority, the National Trust, the volunteers who selflessly do much good work to assist both bodies, the Countryside Commission, the Friends of the Lake District, and the various National Nature Reserves; also to those who have the best interests of the hill walker and mountaineer at heart – the Ramblers' Association, the British Mountaineering Council, the Open Spaces Society, the Climbers' Club and the Fell & Rock Climbing Club. A great deal of appreciation too, must be extended to those conscientious hill farmers who really know and love the land under their tenure and respect it accordingly.

For those who have helped to supply me with equipment a huge thanks to Sue Reay and Martin Geere of Berghaus – whose superb and constantly reliable gear, particularly boots and waterproofs, has kept me unfailingly walking and climbing in all types of extreme conditions. Also thanks to Dave Brown of DB Mountain Sports and Edelrid.

Bill Birkett Photo Library

All the photographs are my own, from the Bill Birkett Photo Library, and are 35mm colour transparencies. Researchers please note that the library holds a huge selection of material covering all of Britain's mountains and wild places, and is one of the most comprehensive available on the English Lake District.

Tel: 015394 37420

e-mail: billbirkett@msn.com

A selection of Berghaus walking equipment

INDEX